ENDORS

So few of us know how to wait well. Ann has lived a long wait and found God in it. We need the vulnerability—laced with the wisdom God has imparted during her years of waiting—that Ann Swindell offers on these pages. As only a skilled storyteller can do, she invites us to find our own stories within hers and within the narrative of Scripture that is written for us, the waiting ones.

SARA HAGERTY
Author of *Every Bitter Thing Is Sweet*

Ann has taken us through a tender, personal journey that we can all relate to. We understand the ache of shame, and we have our own stories of waiting for relief. With biblical truth and the gentle wisdom of a good friend, Ann tells both the Bleeding Woman's story and her own, and leads us to our present hope and fullness in Christ as we wait.

RUTH CHOU SIMONS
Founder of *gracelaced.com*, artist, and author

In *Still Waiting*, Ann gives us insight into what to do while we are waiting. Not only what to do, but how to stay attached to the bigger God-story in the midst of our struggles. Ann has not only given us insight and truth but has lived it out in her own life. May this book stir you to love Jesus more and believe that he is able to meet with you, even in the waiting.

JIMMY SEIBERT
Senior pastor of Antioch Community Church and president of Antioch Ministries International

The remarkable biblical story of the Bleeding Woman whom Jesus healed is the backdrop for this treasure of a book. Weaving in the intimate details of her own ongoing journey to healing with honesty and insight, Ann Swindell creatively, compassionately, and gently takes us by the hand and leads us to Jesus with astonishing wisdom that can only come from personal experience. Her skillfully written words spoke deeply into my often impatient, questioning heart in seasons of waiting, pointing to life-changing truth and providing encouragement and hope. We come to see each element of the waiting as a gift with an eternal purpose, drawing us closer to the one who sovereignly knows our need.

TERRI KRAUS
President of Redbud Writers Guild and author of the
Project Restoration series

Still Waiting offers wisdom and hope in an area I have long struggled to overcome: the ability to wait well. Ann lovingly guides us through Scripture and comes alongside us with her own story as we go on a journey to learn what it means to wait in a way that isn't lazy but provides an open space in our hearts and schedules for God to meet us in the midst of the unknown. And that is always, always, worth the wait.

CRYSTAL STINE
Freelance writer, speaker, and host of the Write 31 Days challenge

Grab a cup of coffee and meet your new best friend. That's how you'll feel after reading this expertly crafted book, which is about far more than waiting. It is about how to live—how to take what life is offering at any moment and be whole and at peace. Swindell intimately weaves together painful and touching stories from her own life with Scripture and reflections, and creates a very real space of hope.

SHAYNE MOORE
Author and founder of Redbud Writers Guild

Ann is passionate, raw, and inviting—on and off the page. Her insight into the life of one woman in the Bible, as it relates to our stories of struggle, carries a mantle of hope and solidarity to those of us waiting on God today.

KAREN STOTT
Founder of Pursuit Community

In *Still Waiting*, both Ann's faith and her struggles are creatively woven together with a biblical story in a way that gives each of us hope for our respective challenges. This is a great reminder of God's faithfulness in spite of our circumstances.

MIKE BAKER
Senior pastor of Eastview Christian Church and author of *Jesus Speaks*

Life constantly (and painfully) reminds us how hard waiting truly is. In fact, waiting may well be one of the most challenging spiritual tasks that's set before us. Ann Swindell gently invites us to learn from someone intimately familiar with waiting: the hemorrhaging woman described in Mark 5. As Ann explores, the short glimpse Scripture gives us of this woman's life and faith is rich fodder for aiding us in our own weakness and waiting, encouraging us to keep reaching out to Jesus in expectant hope.

KELLI B. TRUJILLO
Editor of *CT Women* and author of *The Busy Mom's Guide to Spiritual Survival*

We all have to deal with some degree of waiting in our lives. Through a beautiful retelling of the story of the Bleeding Woman—as well as honest glimpses into her own story—Ann points us back to Jesus in every stage of the waiting process. *Still Waiting* reminds readers that the waiting period can provide fertile soil for our roots to run deep, knowing that our hope lies not in our circumstances but rather in the Lord.

DIANNE JAGO
Founder of *Deeply Rooted* magazine

Ann Swindell tells her story of waiting with winsome honesty. Readers who have fought secret battles will recognize her exhausting effort to avoid shame. Anyone who has prayed the same prayer for years will resonate with her struggle to be content in all circumstances while at the same time holding on to the hope of healing. *Still Waiting* helps the reader not only experience Swindell's story but lift our gaze from her life and our own to the healing love of Christ.

BETSY CHILDS HOWARD
Editor for the *Gospel Coalition*

The way Ann weaves large swaths of Scripture into narrative puts skin on what can seem like just an old Bible story. This book's look at the Bleeding Woman and also Ann's personal testimony provide a strong and welcomed toehold for anyone who has grown tired of waiting as she suffers.

HAYLEY MORGAN
Bestselling author of *Wild and Free* and social entrepreneur

still waiting

HOPE FOR WHEN
GOD DOESN'T GIVE YOU
WHAT YOU WANT

ANN SWINDELL

TYNDALE
MOMENTUM™

*The nonfiction imprint of
Tyndale House Publishers, Inc.*

Visit Tyndale online at www.tyndale.com.

Visit Tyndale Momentum online at www.tyndalemomentum.com.

TYNDALE, Tyndale Momentum, and Tyndale's quill logo are registered trademarks of Tyndale House Publishers, Inc. The Tyndale Momentum logo is a trademark of Tyndale House Publishers, Inc. Tyndale Momentum is the nonfiction imprint of Tyndale House Publishers, Inc., Carol Stream, Illinois.

Still Waiting: Hope for When God Doesn't Give You What You Want

Designed by Ron Kaufmann

Edited by Stephanie Rische

For information about special discounts for bulk purchases, please contact Tyndale House Publishers at csresponse@tyndale.com or call 800-323-9400.

ISBN 978-1-4964-1076-4 Softcover

Printed in the United States of America

23	22	21	20	19	18	17
7	6	5	4	3	2	1

For Michael:
Your love always leads me to Jesus.

CONTENTS

FOREWORD

The other day I hit a breaking point about something. I realized I was being really selfish and silly, and I wasn't trusting God regarding a big old heart issue I was having. I cried, read a bunch of Bible verses, wrote in my journal, and Instagrammed about it—you know, vaguely enough so no one would know specifically about my busted-heart issue. I woke up the next day with the subconscious belief that since I had repented and submitted, God was going to give me my way.

But he didn't. In fact, that day a little salt got into that tiny wound: the heart issue was exacerbated by circumstances totally out of my control. And you'd better believe I wanted to have a spiritual hissy fit—because I had prayed, I had humbled myself, and I had *waited* for a whole eighteen hours for God to do his thing.

The passage of Scripture that's been messing with me the most lately is a really simple verse at the very beginning of Genesis 41. It's smack dab in the thick of Joseph's story of waiting: he has been unjustly imprisoned, and the guy who was supposed to help him out has totally forgotten about him. In Genesis 41:1, the Bible casually mentions, "When two full years had passed . . ." (NIV). Oh, just two years? No biggie. Joseph was just kicking it in jail for two years while life and love and the world passed him by. But I'm over here losing it over my eighteen hours of pain and anguish.

God's people are often called to be a waiting people—not because he is unkind or unloving, but rather the exact opposite. God's people are a waiting people because he is an on-time God, not an on-demand one. So it seems we've got to figure out this waiting thing in a holy and wholehearted way.

We all know we live in a microwave culture—even a microwave *Christian* culture. We can get anything we want, and we can make anything happen, and if someone won't give us what we need, we'll get it from somewhere else— cheaper, faster, and with free shipping too.

But the Lord has never, ever worked this way. And my friend Ann? She knows this. She has lived it. She *is* living it. She has lived his faithfulness, even when it feels like his favor is missing. She has longed to understand his heart, even when she hasn't seen his hand moving. She has grabbed hold of the fruit there is to find in waiting—the fullness of God and the strength of his Spirit.

A good leader goes first, and Ann hasn't just gone first into the tepid waters of waiting; she is also pushing us to receive grace by receiving it herself and telling her story with some brutally beautiful words. Really, she's telling *our* story—as we're all a part of this now-and-not-yet waiting Kingdom of God.

Read on, friends; be blessed; and dive into the grace that waits for *you*.

Jess Connolly

AUTHOR'S NOTE

This book is not, ultimately, a record of my life but a recollection of my journey, so for the sake of time (and your sanity), there are places where I have collapsed or tweaked the timeline in order to save you from confusion and repetitive details. There are also places where I have changed the names of individuals in my story in order to protect them. But the people, events, and places in this book are all real and deeply meaningful to me.

The life of the Bleeding Woman was real too—although Scripture doesn't offer us much in the way of details. I've spent time in the stacks of libraries studying and researching and piecing together the facts that I could about her story, but not many exist. And so, while based on research, much of her narrative—which I offer as a fictional counterpart to my own—is conjecture. We don't know her age when she met Jesus, and we don't know why or how, exactly, she was bleeding. My assumptions in this book are broadly built on the study and suppositions of scholars who have steeped themselves in the realities of the first century. You will find references to many of these texts at the end of the book, if you wish to learn more about her.

Ultimately, my desire is that the story of the Bleeding Woman, along with my own journey, will point you to the truth and goodness of Christ Jesus. He is the reason I set out to write this book in the first place—and why I have a story to tell at all.

A Woman Acquainted with Waiting

There was a woman who had had a discharge of blood for twelve years,
and who had suffered much under many physicians, and had spent all that
she had, and was no better but rather grew worse. She had heard the reports
about Jesus and came up behind him in the crowd and touched his garment.

MARK 5:25-27

The story of the Bleeding Woman has echoed through my life
for years now. I find myself thinking about her, wondering
about her, searching out bits and pieces of her story in theologi-
cal books and commentaries. I want to know who she was and
what her existence was like in the years before she met Jesus.
I want to uncover what her story reveals about the character of
Christ and how he draws near to those who are hurting.

The Bible gives us tiny ribbons of insight into her life. She
had been bleeding for twelve years. She had no money left,
having spent all she had on doctors who were unable to help
her. Physically, she was worse off than she'd ever been before.

And then one interaction with Jesus upended her broken
life and changed everything.

Still, that's about all we know. Braided together, these ribbons offer me a thin rope to climb when it comes to understanding this woman. I don't know her name, I don't know
her age, and I don't even know how her bleeding began.

There are conjectures, theories, and possibilities about her that number to the skies. She remains a mystery.

Yet this mystery helps me identify with her. Where I cannot see her face, I have been able to imagine my own. Where I cannot know her name, I have placed mine between the lines of the Scripture. I have likened myself to the Bleeding Woman.

I do not claim to have experienced the same level of suffering as this woman. I don't know what it's like to bleed for a dozen years with no end in sight or to be ostracized from my community. But her story is, in many ways, a story of waiting—and at the same point in our lives, all of us, like her, find ourselves waiting for something.

I, too, have known years of waiting—years of hoping and praying and dreaming of a cure no doctor could offer, years of waiting for a healing encounter with Jesus. Every new morning was a reminder that I was promised no healing and guaranteed no end stamp on the condition I carried.

Like the Bleeding Woman, I was waiting for Jesus. As I waited, I walked my own journey with God—perhaps similar to the one she lived. No, I didn't walk the same roads or live in the same circumstances, but I asked the same question: Would he give me what I was seeking? As the waiting stretched on, the questions multiplied. Would I still love him, no matter what? Would I still trust him?

It was in the middle of these questions and prayers and confusion that I found myself waiting for a God I couldn't always make sense of or understand.

But I met him *in* the waiting.

And for me, that changed everything.

CHAPTER 1

When Waiting
Makes You Broken

*H*er name, I imagine, was Sarah. A good name—the name of
the wife of Abraham, the father of her people. Her parents
had named her twenty-odd years ago, when she was a tight ball
of legs and arms still grabbing at air, grasping at nothing. She had
been small and sickly when she was born, and they were not sure if
she would make it. So they named her Sarah, hoping that a strong
name would make her strong too.

Whether it was the name or the favor of the God her family
worshiped, Sarah made it through that uncertain first year to
become a healthy, happy little girl. Like other girls in her village,
she stayed home with her mother and learned the work of cleaning
and cooking and telling stories. Her father made respectable money
from his metalworking, and he would arrange for her to marry a

godly man when it was time. Her dowry was fair enough to secure an upright husband, and her father's good name was enough to bring suitors when she was only twelve.

She bled for the first time when she was fourteen. At first, it was cause for quiet celebration in the family—she had reached menses; she had attained womanhood. That week her mother explained to her what she could now expect from her body and what that meant for her in terms of ceremonial purity within the larger community. Each month there would be a time when she would have to stay away from communal worship and the homes of other people. But this was not a punishment; it was simply the way with women.

Then her mother smiled and told Sarah about the future that lay ahead of her. Within the year, she might become betrothed, and within another year or two, she would be wed. Could she imagine, her mother whispered, the joy of having her own children in a few years? Perhaps she might have two children—or three, if God blessed her—before she turned twenty.

Sarah marveled that such a small trickle of blood could change everything. She felt excited about her new status—and happy at her mother's happiness, happy at her father's smile of approval. Life transformed in front of her. Now she was a woman. She would be leaving home soon.

But after two weeks, the bleeding had not stopped. Her mother, who had once been so happy over this news, now started to worry herself around the house. Sarah could tell by the way she kneaded the bread every morning—too much, too hard, too long. Their dinner loaves became misshapen and tired looking. When Sarah asked her mother when the bleeding would stop, her mother told her that it should have stopped already. "Only a week at a time," she said. "Seven days at once, not more."

Sarah did not understand what was going on—in her own body or in her mother's mind.

After three weeks, Sarah overheard her mother talking to her father in low tones after they thought the children had fallen asleep. Sarah shared a mat with her younger sister; her older brothers had already left the house, and her younger brother was only five, heavy with sleep. Sarah heard the fear in her mother's voice, and she strained to understand the words.

The whispers were too low to comprehend, but she knew something was wrong—wrong with her.

The account of the Bleeding Woman is a small story in the Bible, repeated in three of the four Gospels. But it is remarkable in its power and its ability to startle me back to God.

It is the backstory that I daydream about—the life of this woman before her encounter with Christ. To me, that seems to be at least half of the story. The writers of the Gospels note, calmly and evenly, that she had been bleeding for twelve years. But I can't read those lines without wondering about the substance of those days. There was nothing calm or even about those years, I imagine, because not only had she been bleeding for twelve years; she had been *waiting* for twelve years. And waiting is not a calm and even business.

Most of this woman's story in Scripture focuses on her moment with Jesus—that moment of healing, the inversion of her existence. But she had lived through those twelve years, and she suffered through them in ways that are unknown to us. I find myself drawn to those years—drawn to the marrow of them, drawn to the inside of them, drawn to the hurt that must have lingered in every moment of those 4,380 days. Because who but a bleeding woman can know the pain of life leaving your body every moment of the day? Who but a bleeding woman can know the struggle of waiting for a healing that has proven impossible to find?

I am drawn to those years of hers—those days—because I have had years of waiting of my own. Years of brokenness and longing that stretched past twelve.

My own journey unfolds less dramatically than hers—less obviously, perhaps. But it is still full of shame and hiding, still full of the waiting that threatened to undo me.

Where My Story Begins
Like the Bleeding Woman, I grew up immersed in the things of God. Before I was old enough to talk, let alone know any words, I was baptized into Christianity. Held high in a white gown by a pastor in a gray robe, I was sprinkled with water and invited into the life of the church. Not only did that moment signify my parents' vow to raise me in the faith, but it was the first moment of many in my journey toward Christ. Because, as simple as this sounds, I can never remember a day when I haven't loved God. I have always wanted to know him. I still do.

Everything was spiritual to me; I grew up as a deeply attentive child who wanted to see connections running through every flower, every song, every person. I believed that God's presence could be found anywhere, if only I could open my eyes wide enough to see him. I sang songs to God that I made up in my head. I hummed to him as I discovered bark patterns on curving trees in the backyard, and I danced for him as I bent low to smell the strawberry-sweetness that poured from the lilies of the valley splayed across our lawn.

I prayed with childlike fervor, falling asleep with both dreams and fears while trying to understand the concept of eternity. One night, when I was seven or eight years old, I cried for my mother in the dark, terrified that life would go on and on forever. She held me but couldn't give the answer I wanted, because she couldn't explain the unexplainable—that dizzying notion of infinity.

Still, even with my fears and the many things I couldn't comprehend, I continued to pray every night that I can remember. I made recitations to God of my hopes and my thanks, my desires and my wishes. I whispered into the dark of my bedroom, praying in a hush that I trusted he could hear. I believed he was listening.

But also like the Bleeding Woman, my story with suffering—trivial as it might initially seem—starts when I was young. I was eleven. It was an unassuming beginning, something small and originally unmagnified in my life. I was in the school play in fifth grade—*The Pirates of Penzance*. In case you've never heard of the comic opera by Gilbert and Sullivan, it's a tongue-twisting musical that includes pirates, a group of sisters (of whom I was one), and a hero and heroine who fall in love. A classic romance story—with a pirate twist! I loved the music, loved the eyelet dress I got to wear, loved the heat of the lights on my face, loved the rush of color and sound and storytelling swirling around me.

I had been wearing glasses since third grade, but in fifth grade I asked my parents for contacts. They agreed, and I got fitted for gas permeable contact lenses—a long name for hard contacts. Every morning I tucked the tiny plastic disks over my pupils, feeling them swim and settle onto the centers of my eyes. Every evening I diligently popped them out, cleaned them, and snapped them into my contact case. Click, click.

What happened during those months in fifth grade before *The Pirates of Penzance* is that I developed a fascination with my eyes—particularly, with my eyelashes and eyebrows. When showtime came, I applied theater makeup, which included mascara. I had never worn makeup before, and adding mascara to my lashes created another layer of captivation with my eyes. I started touching my eyelashes and running the tips of my fingers along them. My eyelashes were long and very full; I had inherited them from my father. They were lovely.

It happened during one performance as I stood in the tiled hallway: I waited for my cue to enter (stage left), and I pulled out my first eyelash. I remember the moment, remember the feeling. It felt good, like the release of a sneeze. It felt like the pop that comes from unscrewing a pressurized jar. It felt like the start of something I didn't understand.

That day I plucked out my first eyelash and, although I didn't know it at the time, started a habit that snowballed into years and years of pulling out my own eyelashes and eyebrows.

It is odd, I know. It is strange.

What started as a passing moment avalanched a deep struggle into my young life. After that, I pulled out eyelashes every day. Every single day.

It felt like a release of tension; it felt like I couldn't stop. At first, I don't remember my parents noticing that I was pulling out my eyelashes, and later, my eyebrows. I didn't think too much about it either. But soon the bare patches of skin framing my eyes became visibly obvious.

I didn't know what was happening, and my parents seemed to be as mystified as I was. They would tell me to stop playing with my eyelashes, to stop touching them. I would tell myself the same thing. But even though I didn't like what I was doing—even though I hated how it made me look— I found that I couldn't stop. When I felt a little stressed or uncomfortable or slightly anxious—a tendency passed down through my genes—my hands would start floating up to my lash line, ready to pluck out a lash or two. Or three or four.

But I didn't always pull out my lashes just because I leaned toward perfectionism as a child, just because I was prone to low-grade anxiety. Sometimes I tugged on my lash line when I wasn't thinking, wasn't worried, wasn't stressed. I've always been a reader, and I would spend hours on our family room couch, diving into rich worlds on the page, devouring whole books and series over the course of a few days.

The problem? I found that every time I read, the pages of my books were covered with eyelashes. Tiny brown Cs, peppered like unwanted snowflakes across the pages. I cried when I saw them; I didn't know how to stop doing what I didn't want to do. My parents cried with me; they didn't know how to stop me either.

And so they started doing some research. My father, a physician, discovered that what I was struggling with was a real condition, odd as it seemed.

The diagnosis: a medical condition called trichotillomania. It turned out I wasn't the only one with an itching desire to pull out my eyelashes and my eyebrows; it actually had a name. Some people pull hair from their heads or from their arms; I pulled out my eyelashes and brows. Trichotillomania, as we came to find out, is fairly common—it's estimated that up to 4 percent of people across the globe and one percent of Americans (or about 2.5 million people in the United States) live with the condition.[1] But it remains mostly unknown to the general public, and chances are, you've never even heard of it. That's because it is rarely discussed. Why?

Shame. That's why.

How do you explain to someone that you can't stop pulling out your own hair? How do you say that what you feel is like a gravitational pull—although no one is forcing you to do the thing that you hate? How could I explain that in my brain, the urge to pull on—and out—my eyelashes was a low-level earthquake constantly rumbling below the surface?

I couldn't. It was too strange, too weird.

Imagine it for yourself: you aren't pulling out your hair in a dramatic display of biblical despair, as Ezra did when he learned that the people of God were disobeying Yahweh (see Ezra 9:3). You aren't shaving it off as a mourning ritual, as Job did (see Job 1:20). Your hair isn't falling out due to old age or chemotherapy—both socially acceptable reasons for losing hair. You alone are responsible for pulling out your hair, for ruining your own appearance. And as much as you want to stop, you find it to be impossible.

Unlike self-harm, trichotillomania is a medical diagnosis that isn't necessarily based in self-hate—although many sufferers report feelings of low self-esteem due to their condition. *The American Journal of Psychiatry* defines the condition this way:

> Trichotillomania is a poorly understood disorder
> characterized by repetitive hair pulling that leads
> to noticeable hair loss, distress, and social or
> functional impairment. The peak age at onset is
> 12–13 years, and the disorder is often chronic and
> difficult to treat. . . . In DSM-IV, it is categorized
> as an impulse control disorder. . . . Although rising
> tension and subsequent pleasure, gratification, or
> relief are integral to the current diagnostic criteria
> for trichotillomania, many people with debilitating
> hair pulling do not endorse these criteria.[2]

So this urge I had to pull out my lashes as a little girl? This inability to stop? It was textbook behavior. But as my father continued to research, he also discovered that according to most sources, trichotillomania is incurable. Medical books told him it was unexplainable. Some of his fellow doctors said it was permanent.

It is difficult, if not impossible, to treat. There is no cure.

Some people with trich start pulling due to trauma, either familial or physical: the divorce of parents, the death of a pet, even a move to a new town. I dealt with none of these things. I had a stable home life, loving parents, and a fun little sister. I struggled for a while with my weight, but other than that, my biggest trauma had been that Peter didn't want to date me in fourth grade. Yes, I was a little on the worrisome and anxious side—I always wanted to do things right, and well. But my onset of trich had no clear medical reason, and now apparently my diagnosis had no clear solution.

I wonder if this is, in some small way, how the Bleeding Woman felt. There was no clear reason for the onset of her bleeding—at least, not that we know about. There was no clear solution for how to treat it or how to fix it. There was no direction at all. Just a physical, shameful, confusing problem that led to days of waiting and then years of waiting—waiting for a cure that never materialized. It would take a miracle for her to be healed.

It would take a miracle for me to be healed too.

The Brokenness We Bear
All of us live with brokenness in our lives. To varying degrees and in various ways, brokenness is more normal than foreign in the human experience. And although I know there were many other ways I was already broken as an eleven-year-old, trichotillomania was the clearest way I started to understand brokenness in myself. Up until that point, I had been a "good girl": I did what I was supposed to do, I finished my homework assignments, I sang loudly in the church choir, I ate my

veggies. And I genuinely liked being a good girl—I've always been a rule follower by nature, another soul in a long line of rule followers on both sides of my family. Like my parents and grandparents and great-grandparents before me, I felt secure when I did the right thing. This way of living offered me a sense of internal control.

But with trichotillomania, suddenly I couldn't do what I believed was the right thing. That insatiable compulsion to pull out my eyelashes and eyebrows—and the fact that I kept pulling them out, even when I wanted to stop—made me *feel* broken. That was the first time I experienced the emotion of knowing my own brokenness. It was also the first time I felt helpless to change my brokenness. Even though I wished and hoped and prayed it would disappear, trich wouldn't leave me alone.

It felt like a blot on my young life, like a red X on what had previously been a perfect test. Up until the age of eleven, if I'd had real brokenness, I'd been able to effectively ignore it or mask it. That Koosh ball I stole from my cousin as a five-year-old? I apologized and never did it again. That mean thing I said to my little sister? I stopped saying it. But when it came to trich, I couldn't stop. I couldn't *ever* stop. My parents couldn't fix it, and I couldn't fix it. *Stuck* isn't a strong enough word to explain how I felt. *Trapped* comes closer. Ultimately, when it came down to it, the only thing I could do was wait—and hope that I might grow out of trichotillomania.

In ways both small and overwhelming, we all know what brokenness feels like. And sometimes our own brokenness—or the brokenness of those we love—seems like too much to bear. Whether it's buying more than we can afford or striking out in anger at the people we love or eating more than we want to or pushing people away when we need them most, we all have places where brokenness is painfully apparent in our own hearts. We all have parts of our lives where we are waiting for things to change.

Whether we're waiting for physical healing or emotional wholeness or spiritual breakthrough, we are all waiting for our brokenness to be mended. We wait because we are broken, and we are broken because we are waiting.

We wait because we are broken.

What we know in our bones is also declared in the Bible: all creation is tattered, destroyed, and torn. And it has been since that first act of rebellion in the Garden of Eden. The decision Adam and Eve made to disobey God toppled the perfection in that place, and ever since, everything around us—and everything within us—has been damaged by sin and death. All creation groans for renewal:

> The creation waits with eager longing for the revealing
> of the sons of God. For the creation was subjected to
> futility, not willingly, but because of him who subjected
> it, in hope that the creation itself will be set free from
> its bondage to corruption and obtain the freedom of
> the glory of the children of God. For we know that the
> whole creation has been groaning together in the pains
> of childbirth until now. And not only the creation,

but we ourselves, who have the firstfruits of the Spirit, groan inwardly as we wait eagerly for adoption as sons, the redemption of our bodies.

ROMANS 8:19-23

The world itself is in a season of waiting, of groaning, of yearning for completion. Brokenness is all around us. Yes, one day God will come and make everything new. But until then, we wait in the brokenness. What we cannot secure on our own—ultimate peace, physical health, environmental abundance—we wait for from the hand of God.

We are broken because we are waiting. At any point, God could end the waiting. He could renew all things in a moment. But he hasn't done so yet—and we don't know when he will. Until then, we are the waiting ones—the ones who are betting it all on a God who saves, on a God who promises to come through. For as long as he prolongs his coming, we remain broken. And yet—*and yet*—even his prolonging is a kindness. He prolongs his coming because he is patient:

Do not overlook this one fact, beloved, that with the Lord one day is as a thousand years, and a thousand years as one day. The Lord is not slow to fulfill his promise as some count slowness, but is patient toward you, not wishing that any should perish, but that all should reach repentance. But the day of the Lord will come like a thief, and then the heavens will

pass away with a roar, and the heavenly bodies will
be burned up and dissolved, and the earth and the
works that are done on it will be exposed.

2 PETER 3:8-10

The day is coming—coming like a thief—when the waiting will finally be over. Until then, though, we remain broken. And so we must learn to love this patient God in the
waiting and in our own brokenness.

We know the defeat of broken waiting.
Having trichotillomania as a child made me feel sad and sorry
and broken in a way I hadn't known yet. This was a brokenness so persistent that I couldn't escape it, not even for a day.
I knew Jesus then, even loved him. But I didn't know what
difference he was making in this part of my life. Although I
prayed for him to take away my condition, he didn't seem to
be hearing that particular prayer. While my little life looked
squeaky clean from the outside, there was one segment of my
life I couldn't gain mastery over: I couldn't be good enough
to will trichotillomania away.

I remember sitting on the blue leather couch in the family
room of our old house, my legs stretched out over the three
cushions, pretending to be reading when I was really just
counting the eyelashes on the page.

Seven, eight, nine.

I didn't have words then, at the age of eleven, to name
what I was feeling. But what I was feeling was *defeated*.
Completely defeated. Like an utter failure.

Maybe you know the feeling. Maybe your body has betrayed you, or maybe your family is falling apart. Maybe you're reeling from a broken heart or the sting of professional rejection. Maybe you struggle with the pain of unmet dreams and shelved goals that might never happen.

Whatever it is and wherever it comes from, we all know the hollow truth of brokenness, of feeling defeated, of seeing ourselves as failures.

Looking for a Miracle

As I write this, I am in the midst of Holy Week. And like any Easter where I live, Resurrection Day comes between winter and spring.

It is April in Chicagoland, and this past weekend was lovely. It was warm enough to wear a T-shirt and shorts, and I was actually able to forgo what has been my constant companion for the last half a year—a cardigan. Although my sister teases me about my cardigan collection, I love the truth of a cardigan: it does what it advertises, shielding me from the biting wind that sinks its teeth into Chicago even on the days when the sun has come out.

Still, even with the cardigan gone this weekend, after so many months of winter it's hard to have faith that spring is actually on its way. It's easier to believe that I've been cold forever—and that I *will* be cold forever. The cold has swirled around me so long that I've nearly forgotten warmth; even the air has smelled stripped and sterile, devoid of life and abundance.

But this past weekend I actually wondered if spring might

fight its way through the chill and the cold that has settled in my bones. The sun and the warmth this past Friday and Saturday gave me a taste of spring—and with it, the hope that winter might truly be over.

Then yesterday, after a weekend of seventy-five-degree days, it snowed. And it didn't just snow for minutes. It snowed for hours. *Hours.* In April. White, crystalline snow, piling on the bushes and in the pockets of newly blossomed tulip leaves like tiny white anthills. The clouds came back, and the sky turned gray. The sun was nowhere to be found.

So I did what I had to do: I shut every blind and closed every door and sat in denial inside my house. I couldn't bear to see it again, this fight between winter and spring. I couldn't watch the snow beat back the flowers that were just daring to bloom. The flowers wouldn't make it. The tulips and the daffodils that had worked so hard to fight through the earth and blossom—now they would die.

And I remember, here in this Holy Week, that thousands of years ago, something similar happened, but on a scale much grander and greater. It appeared that Jesus might be coming into the spring of his own life and ministry. He performed miracles, raised people from the dead, gained a following. The shouts rang out like bells as people welcomed him into Jerusalem, lifting palm branches and flinging their coats under the hooves of the colt he rode.

But suddenly the winter of Maundy Thursday and Good Friday came upon him. The events that transpired on these days—both of them—were heart wrenching. Betrayal, abandonment, false witness, political mongering, beating, whipping, spitting, splitting, breaking, bleeding. These days marked a sudden turn back to winter and death. Jesus, hanging on the cross: the flower of his life beaten back by a darkness so great he bled and died.

Jesus bled too.

He knows what it's like to have blood leave the body in great rivers, in unstoppable streams.

He knows the reality of being ostracized. He knows what it is to have no way out of his circumstances. He knows what it is to be broken, in his heart and in his limbs. His body pulverized. His spirit abandoned. He knows what it is to wait for God to come through—and to die in the waiting.

I dare not write about brokenness and pain, about weakness and shame, or about the difficulty of waiting without turning first to the Cross. My struggle with trichotillomania as a child, the brokenness of the Bleeding Woman, the sorrow of unmet desires, the pain any of us walk through and with—all of it is found in that torn man on the cross. And in the death he died.

The Resurrection will come, and with it every promise of healing and wholeness will be fulfilled. But there is no guarantee that we'll experience that resurrection wholeness until the final return of our Lord. And so, until that day, all of us find ourselves in a season of waiting—the waiting between Jesus' going and his coming. The waiting between the groaning of creation and the day when all things are made new. The waiting between all of this pain, suffering, death, and destruction, and the time when every tear will be wiped away.

In one way or another, all of us find ourselves in the meta-
phorical hours between Friday and Sunday, because we are all
waiting in some way. Waiting for test results, waiting for our
marriage to turn a corner, waiting for a job that pays the bills,
waiting for our child to return to God, waiting for healing,
waiting for hope. Waiting.

Like the Bleeding Woman who needed a miracle, all of
us need one too.

We are waiting for Jesus to swing his robe wide enough
to grasp it, that we might be made whole.

CHAPTER 2

When Waiting
Makes You Weak

The bleeding would not stop.

Sarah's mother threaded her through town until they entered into the house of the oldest midwife in the village. Her simple home held a table in the middle of the room, and Sarah noticed a birthing chair in the corner. But she did not look around much; she focused on the dirt on the floor, trying to avoid her mother's face. The shame she felt from her mother made her ashamed too, and when the midwife asked her what her illness was, she found no courage to speak. Her mother spoke for her, hushing her voice although no one else was around.

The midwife nodded and looked at Sarah. The tenderness she saw in the old woman's eyes surprised her.

"She is young. Sometimes the body is confused at the first sign

of menses. She will be fine. Give her another month, and see if she regulates. If she does not, then you should see a physician. But I do not think that will be necessary."

Sarah felt some of the fear lift and even caught the edge of a hopeful smile on her mother's face. *Perhaps she really would be all right? Perhaps nothing was actually wrong?*

But three months and several doctor appointments later, Sarah was still bleeding.

It was not heavy, but there was a constant trickle of blood every day. Every night her mother asked her whether the bleeding had stopped, and Sarah started to hate the approach of sundown. She knew that once again she would disappoint the hope her mother was still harboring.

Eventually, her mother stopped asking.

Meanwhile, Sarah grew tired, unendingly tired. By the time the sun hit midday, she was exhausted. When her morning chores around the house were completed, she would often sleep for an hour or two until the heat of the day passed. And no matter the time of day, she felt weak. So very weak. Her siblings did not need an afternoon nap; only the very young or the very old needed such sleep. Sarah was embarrassed by her incessant need to rest.

Actually, she realized one day, floating in and out of consciousness while the sun flamed the afternoon sky, she felt embarrassed about everything. She always felt weak and tired, and she hated how often she needed to ask her mother if she could return to her mat after one chore. She was embarrassed about her inability to marry, about her consistent bleeding, about being incessantly unclean.

The sun seared her vision. Yes, that was it. Sarah was embarrassed to be alive.

As I hit my junior high years—twelve, thirteen, fourteen—I couldn't stop pulling out my eyelashes. I kept waiting for a day when I would wake up and finally be done with trich. It never came.

And so the patchiness in my lash line grew worse. Sometimes, for short bursts, I would have a week or two where I'd pull out only one or two eyelashes a day, and then my lash line would fill in—haltingly, sparsely. Those were the easier weeks and months, when my trich wasn't so glaringly apparent, at least to my parents and my sister. I couldn't even bring myself to wonder if any of my classmates realized that I didn't have "normal" eyelashes or eyebrows; I tried not to think about it. I wasn't wearing makeup yet, except for special occasions, and I didn't have any way to hide what I was doing to myself.

I doubt that any child could have grown up in as loving a home as I did; my parents were unendingly affectionate and generous with my sister and me. I don't remember a day of my life when my mother didn't tell me she loved me and that she was glad I was her daughter. She had named all of her childhood dolls Ann; I always knew I was wanted and loved and cherished. Similarly, I don't remember a day of my life when my father didn't tell me how proud he was of me or that he loved me or that I was beautiful. Even now that I am solidly into adulthood, my father exclaims when I am home to visit, "I think you're getting prettier as you're getting older!" And I smile and hug him—because I know he truly means it, and I know he sees me through the eyes of fatherly love.

I have always adored my parents, and I have always wanted to please them. C. S. Lewis writes in his essay "The Weight of Glory" about "the specific pleasure of . . . a child before its father," when the child experiences deep satisfaction simply in pleasing him. As Lewis describes, this is the end delight of the redeemed soul—to please "Him whom she was created to please."[1] In our best moments, we are content—yes, even thrilled—to make our heavenly Father happy, just as children are thrilled to make their parents happy. And perhaps because of that innate desire I've always felt to please the parents who loved me so well, my struggle with trich was the first time in my life that I felt like a disappointment. Not because they were disappointed in me—they never said or did anything to make me feel that way. In fact, now that I'm a parent myself, I realize they probably suffered more for me than I did for myself; such is the love of a parent for a child. But I felt like a disappointment because it was the first time I simply couldn't *get it together*. I couldn't will myself to be better or whole or healed. And I felt that in letting myself down, I was letting them down too.

My father is a tall man—a few inches above six feet. Although I've grown to his shoulders now, when I was a child he was a towering tree in front of me. It seemed that he encompassed all the strength and warmth I could ever need.

22

ANN SWINDELL

But his height also meant that while my peers might look me in the face—or even look up to me, since I was often one of the tallest students in my grade—my father always looked down at me. And one particular day as we stood and talked in the kitchen, I realized that he was looking down at my eyelashes, checking to see how I was doing with trich. I knew already: I was doing badly. I was always doing badly. He was a physician, and he saw the world through the lens of a healer. He looked at me with eyes of compassion and curiosity. He wanted to help—he wanted to heal. But all I could think in that moment was that he was seeing how much damage I had done to myself, and all I could feel was how much I had failed. I looked down at the terrazzo floor in the kitchen, a whirl of orange and red and gray, overcome with sadness that I wasn't healed. I was sad for myself, yes, but I was also sad for my dad.

It wasn't that my father was critical; he didn't chastise me or reprimand me. I don't think he even mentioned my eyelashes that day. I am sure, however, that he gave me a hug—because that's what he always did. But I remember standing under his gaze—I remember that feeling of being caught red-handed in front of the very person I wanted to please. And I felt—how else to put it?—embarrassed. When my father looked at my eyelashes that day, I knew what he would see, and I was embarrassed. I felt like a disappointment.

And so I told myself, over and over, that I should get it together. Certainly I could muscle my way through this, get tougher on myself, try harder. Why was I so weak in the one area I wanted to be strong? *Get it together, Ann!* That's what I

23

thought and spoke over myself ten or twenty or thirty times a day. When I ripped out an eyelash: *Just stop it, Ann!* When I yanked out another one: *Why can't I just pull myself together?* When I tugged out an eyebrow hair: *I'm such a failure! How will I ever get over this?* When I had to put down a book because I'd already pulled out five, ten, fifteen lashes: *Why am I so weak? Why can't I get over this?*

I saw weakness as an obstacle to get around. Or push through. Or ignore. Maybe it's because I'm competitive. Maybe it's because I'm stubborn. But I've never liked feeling weak, and even today I try to avoid that emotion whenever I can.

I've always been this way, even before trich. As a young child, I thrived on knowing the answers in class, and I always wanted to win HORSE in PE. I tried out for musicals in elementary school, loving the moments under the bright lights, even if just for a few minutes as a supporting character (thus, *The Pirates of Penzance*).

And in junior high, those same years when embarrassment about my struggle with trich was settling in, I was known as one of the toughest girls on the basketball court. Not because I was particularly strong; I was a waif in those years, growing taller than the rest of my body could keep up with (don't worry: puberty quickly made up for that stage). But my competitiveness on the basketball court meant that I was more than willing to hurl my body onto the floor for a loose ball.

Our coach ran a drill specifically to teach us to let go of our desire to stay vertical. "'The goal is to get the ball before she does," he would shout, while all of us were lined up at center court. "Whatever it takes, you get that ball first. I'm not worried about fouling right now. I'm worried about *heart*. Get that ball!"

Two at a time, we would step up to the half-court line before he rolled the basketball—*fast*—toward the free throw line. The player who gained control of the ball got to stay in for another round. There was no punching allowed, although kicking and elbowing were the norm. It was a game of last girl standing.

And often, I was the girl who was left. My knees were bruised from here to Kane County, but I wasn't going to let anyone else get that ball. If it meant throwing my body across the court or ripping the ball out of the other girl's hands or knocking my kneecaps on the hardwood—I would do it. I wanted to be strong and capable. And most of the time, I was. Not only on the court but also with friends and in the classroom. I liked people, and (when I wasn't scrambling on the basketball court) I was a nice kid. I made and kept friends easily. I valued school and enjoyed nearly every subject but math. I sang in the school choir and landed the occasional solo. In most areas in my life, I was left standing. And I gained a lot of confidence from those successes.

But not with trich. With trich, I was always slammed down.

Always, always, I was trying to stop my hands from reaching for my eyes. And I know what you might be thinking: *When you see your hands lifting toward your eyes, put them back down. Just stop.*

It wasn't that easy. It was never that easy.

I tried every conceivable idea to overcome my struggle with trich.

First, I wore goggles. My dad tinkered with lots of tools in the basement, and he had protective eyewear—large plastic goggles that he kept in the basement for potentially hazardous work. These goggles were tinted amber, bulky, nearly square on the face; they were made for adult men.

Me? I wore them around the house, trying to create a shield between my hands and my lashes. They were much too big for my small face; they constantly slipped down my nose. But I tried.

I went to see a counselor, who recommended that I try behavior modification in the form of a rubber band. Whenever I was home, I wore a thick, tan-colored band around my wrist. Every time I pulled out a lash—*snap*. It stung like an errant spark from the fire, but it wasn't enough. The urge to wrestle out my lashes always overrode the pain of that rubber band sting. Therapy didn't work. But I tried.

I held modeling clay in my hands while I read or did homework in an attempt to distract my hands from rising like wayward window shades, always going up and up and up and up. I tried.

I wore winter gloves in the house, even in the summer, thinking that if I sheathed my hands, they might quit their pulling. I tried.

But it seemed I never tried hard enough; I never could make it work. The goggles would slip off, and my hand would be at the ready, by my lash line. The rubber band never hurt enough to change the pattern my neurons were carving in my brain to *pull, pull, pull.* The clay would eventually be put down, the gloves would get too hot, and I was back at square one, trying but always failing in this one thing I could not seem to succeed in. My weakness, it seemed, was insurmountable.

Weakness and Wonder

As much as those years were full of struggle, they were also marked by the kindness of God, and my relationship with him was blossoming. Two parallel tracks ran through my life: one track of joy, one of constant disappointment. While I don't have any memory of my life without Jesus in it, there were varying degrees of my awareness of and desire for him, and it was in junior high when I came to terms with my deep, unyielding need for Christ.

I had started attending a new church—one where the youth group was vibrant and engaged and hilariously fun. The youth leader and his wife—they were just *made* to do youth ministry. You know the type? Someone who can simultaneously kick back with tweens and talk about the deep things of God in the same hour? These people are walking miracles. Looking back, now, I want to hug every junior high pastor in the world; is there ever a cross section of humanity as odd and tender as a junior high girl in the same room with a junior high boy?

It was during my Wednesday nights at youth group, between water balloon fights and chubby bunny contests, that I heard the gospel afresh. And there in that carpet-padded auditorium every Wednesday night, I came to grasp the truth that nothing in my life would make any sense if Jesus wasn't at the center of it. I needed Jesus. While I already knew him as my Savior, these were the years when I was starting to learn what it meant to know him as my Lord.

So I did what any twelve-year-old girl does when she's wrestling with deep thoughts. I went shopping.

A Christian bookstore had recently opened in our town, and every week I pleaded with my parents to drive me there so I could mill around the teenage book section. The titles were fantastic. Some of my favorites included the following:

- *Guys and a Whole Lot More: Advice for Teen Girls on Almost Everything!*
- *Bad Girls of the Bible*
- *Lockers, Lunch Lines, Chemistry, and Cliques*
- *Stuff You Don't Have to Pray About*

But I was twelve, and puberty hadn't kicked in yet for me. Boys were still mostly gross, and I wasn't interested in them or in bad girls like Delilah. What I did want was to pray more, and better. I wanted to *learn* how to pray. I found one book called *Lord, I Haven't Talked to You since the Last Crisis, But...* and flipped through it. The book was full of chapters that let me fill in the blanks for prayers that would be helpful to pray. There was a prayer to pray when I was angry, a prayer for when I was sad, and one for when I was feeling thankful. Since I was already a reading nerd, this seemed the perfect fusion of my love for reading and my desire to learn how to pray better. I devoured the book, filling in the blanks and reading prayers to God for the next month. I didn't tell anyone about the hours I spent writing out my prayers when I got home from school, but this was one of my favorite parts of the day.

And it was during this time that my first memory of experiencing Jesus—actually feeling him with me—took place. I had just been praying out of my fill-in-the-blank book, and I left my room to walk into our family room.

All at once, I was aware of the fact that Jesus was with me, in that little hallway next to the pink bathroom. I looked behind me to make sure it wasn't my little sister. It wasn't. I stood in place, as still as I could. The wood paneling in the hallways muted the light, and everything around me was quiet. I knew that Jesus was with me; he was standing next to me. I couldn't see him, but I could sense him, and his presence made me feel safe and calm. I think I smiled.

When nothing happened for several seconds, I kept walking, wondering if he was going to stay with me. He did. I kept walking down the hallway and into our family room with the navy couches and the worn rug, and slowly—slowly—my sensing of his nearness wore off. I paced into the kitchen, grabbed a cracker, and munched for a minute. I couldn't feel Jesus anymore, but something inside me had shifted. I knew he was going to go with me. Everywhere. He hadn't said anything. I just knew.

That wonder-filled moment in the hallway marked my junior high years of faith in Jesus. I made real friends who were also learning to love God, and we went to Christian concerts, on a church service trip, and to each other's houses for hangouts and laugh sessions.

Those were precious years for me; I found that the deeper I went into Jesus, the more there was to him, to his love and kindness. It was like digging in dry sand: as I pitched myself into God, a thousand bits of his goodness filled up every place inside me. His love met my desires and my wonderings, even as I dug deeper into myself and deeper into him.

And yet trich still colored my daily experience. What felt like a small habit became increasingly difficult to ignore. I couldn't go through a day of school or an hour of homework without pulling out multiple eyelashes. Underneath all the good things in my young life, there was this thread that kept tugging at everything else: the nagging feeling of constantly failing.

Some days when the thread wasn't yanked too hard, I could disregard it for the most part and go about my life. But other days that thread of failure was tugged so strongly that it pulled everything else taut, making the rest of my life feel stretched thin. Although I succeeded in many areas, the continual failure of pulling out my eyelashes and eyebrows marked most days as a letdown. And what I can now identify as low-grade anxiety—probably part of the reason why I developed trich in the first place—birthed more anxiety. The worse I was doing, the worse I did. Anxiety bred anxiety, and for me, hair pulling bred more hair pulling.

It felt like there was a disconnect between what I was learning about Jesus—the goodness and love I was experiencing

at church, at home, through prayer, and with my friends—
and what I was experiencing with trich every day. Although
Jesus was starting to impact every area of my life in meaningful ways, trich was the one thing he didn't seem to help
me with. I knew he was strong; I knew he was the King. But
my struggle with trich made me feel so very weak—a feeling
I didn't like at all. No matter how often I asked him to, it
didn't seem that Jesus was going to take this struggle away.
On top of that, my trich wasn't getting better. It was only
getting worse.

When You Can't Muscle Through

As humans who live in a broken world, we come to know
weakness the same way we come to know a new scar on our
flesh: what is at first unfamiliar and new eventually becomes
normal, consistent, even expected.

And, like a scar that won't go away, I have found that it
has gotten harder and harder to ignore my weaknesses. I'm
not in junior high anymore, and although weaknesses are still
present in my life, they tend to be less clear-cut—and more
potent. My tendency, still, is to try to hide them. Or ignore
them. Neither works very well.

As I sit here typing, my temples are throbbing with a
headache. And while it's not always a headache, the reality is
that most of my days are filled with varying types of weakness. Many I have been living with for years, and some are
the kinds of weaknesses that still startle and surprise me: my
own temper flaring after a night with little sleep, the way I
reach for a chocolate bar when I'm feeling discouraged. But

always, always, I have my fists clenched in front of my face, trying to fend off these weaknesses that threaten to bring me down or trip me up.

I have spent much of my life trying to sidestep my weaknesses. I want to be strong. I want to be capable. And from the outside, I suppose others could look at my life and notice only—or mostly—the strengths. I have been married for a decade, and my husband, who has pastored and is now in seminary, is a wonderful man. I completed my MFA in writing—the terminal degree in my field—and got to teach at my alma mater as a visiting instructor of English. Now I am writing a book and teaching other writers online. We have a bright, beautiful daughter, and she is healthy. My parents recently celebrated their fortieth anniversary.

On paper, my life stacks up well. But the underbelly of these things is that all of them are riddled with weakness. My husband has been fighting significant health issues for much of our marriage, and we have both been exhausted by it. Church life has been meaningful but difficult, and the delicacy of friendships as a pastor's wife has been a place of constant growth and, often, pain. I was wait-listed before getting into my MFA program and felt mostly inadequate while I was there. I was the lowest on the totem pole in the department where I taught, just above an adjunct professor. My pregnancy was the hardest thing I've ever faced, and the thought of becoming pregnant again terrifies me. My parents are getting unavoidably old, and their bodies are starting to break down.

These are the things that I don't talk about often.

Honestly, I try not to *think* about these things often. But the weaknesses are there, always.

In my junior high years, trichotillomania was a weakness that I could never get away from. It was consistently this area of my life that I couldn't muscle through. Trich was a daily reminder that I was weak and that I couldn't just get it together, try as I did with goggles and gloves and modeling clay. I couldn't wiggle my way out of that weakness, that brokenness—and I couldn't ignore it. My failure in that area was an unrelenting reminder of my personal, constant weakness. For a capable kid to not be able to keep her hands away from her eyes, to not be able to stop pulling out her own eyelashes? It felt embarrassing. It felt humiliating.

Where Weakness Leads Us

I'm guessing that weakness was humiliating for the Bleeding Woman, too. The blood itself was a daily sign of her brokenness, and the weakness that followed all that blood loss was an added insult to a very obvious injury. Not only was she unable to participate in the daily life of the community because of her bleeding (her bleeding rendered her unclean and unable to be in holy places or even to touch others, lest she contaminate them), but she also may have been too tired to do much for herself. Sick and tired. It's what we all loathe.

Simply put, she must have been exhausted. The loss of blood, over years and years, would have taken a great toll on her. The human body is amazing in its capacity to replace what we lose—more hair, more saliva, more tears, more blood. But it takes energy to make blood, and we aren't made to have a constant trickle—or flow—of blood dripping out of our bodies for thousands of days.

During that first trimester when my daughter was growing inside me, I remember the surprising fatigue that would drape over me like a thick fog—sometimes as early as ten in the morning. I panted after taking a flight of stairs too quickly, my mouth hanging open like a puppy. It was astounding, really; just weeks before I'd been running four miles without breathing (too) heavily. But as a pregnant woman, I could nap on command, and the taskmaster was my own body, demanding ridiculous amounts of sleep. Even apart from the vomiting, nausea, and utter malaise, underneath everything I was just *tired.* Dog tired, dead on my feet, pooped—pick your cliché, I was living it. I would often teach my morning class at the college and then go home to nap for an hour so I could make it through teaching my afternoon class. I felt ridiculously wimpy.

My body was doing an amazing thing, yes—building thousands of cells that were morphing into my daughter's lungs and ears and strong, beating heart. But part of the reason I was so utterly exhausted stems from the other work my body was doing: making blood. During pregnancy, a woman's blood volume increases by approximately 20–50 percent; my body was creating lots and lots of blood.

We don't know how much blood the Bleeding Woman was losing every day, but there's a reason why they make you sit for twenty minutes and eat a cookie after you donate blood—they know your body will be tired and trying to recalibrate after giving so much away. They keep you seated so you don't faint. They feed you sugary foods to offer your body access to some quick calories—and energy. So even if the Bleeding Woman was losing a small trickle every day, her body was constantly working overtime to keep up with the blood loss. Most of us never lose blood, except possibly during a monthly period. And honestly? I'm tired then, too. Most likely the Bleeding Woman was anemic—her chronic blood loss would have probably created an iron deficiency in her body that she could never completely make up.[2] The common side effects of chronic anemia are numerous: fatigue, headache, shortness of breath, hair loss, tongue soreness, even ringing in the ears.[3]

The Bleeding Woman probably felt weary every day for those twelve years. Weakness was her constant companion. She knew the lassitude in her bones, and there was no end in sight. I imagine that she fought against the creeping fatigue for a while and tried to be strong—it's our tendency as women, our tendency as humans. But eventually, when her condition refused to end, the Bleeding Woman would have had to accept her weakness as a constant part of her life and figure out ways to live with and around it. Still, I can imagine she was embarrassed. I can imagine that she struggled and that she hated the weakness that coursed through her veins.

All of us, from the oldest person alive down to the youngest baby catching her breath for the first time, know weakness. We know it in gradations, of course. Some of us face weakness from the womb—physical or mental weakness that we may never be free from this side of heaven. Some of us don't experience real backbreaking weakness until we are older. But whether it's physical or familial or emotional, it catches us unaware and sends us groping in the dark.

Weakness comes in many forms: bruised kneecaps, wounded hearts, bare lashes, blood. Whatever form it comes in, we all face weakness. We can't escape it, whether it makes its appearance through the betrayal of our bodies or the betrayal of our minds. The shins that start aching after every run. The anxiety that clambers to the surface every time we drop our kids off at school or look at the bank account or step on the scale. The marriage that unravels, the child who refuses to open up his heart to us. The friend who lets us down when we need her most.

As a kid, I wanted to run away from the weakness of trich, push it aside, plow it over. I didn't like weakness, because it started forcing me to the edge of myself. There, at the chasm between where I was and where I wanted to be, was my weakness, my inability to fix what I didn't like in my own life. If I wanted to do better in math at school, I simply worked harder, and the solution eventually came (with some tutoring help from my dad). If I wanted to be a starter on the basketball team, I worked on my shot and my rebounding; the skills eventually developed. But not with trich. Trich forced me to look into the cavern of myself and experience the fear of not being able to cross over to the other side. I couldn't fix it.

And in that place of wanting to be healed but unable to make myself better, I had to stop trying. I had to wait.

Let me put it more honestly: I was *forced* to wait. I didn't want to have to wait for God to heal me—I wanted to be able to do something on my own, whether that was use behavior modification or don protective eyewear. Those weren't bad things, but they never helped me, and eventually I had no other choice: I had to wait for someone stronger than I was to move on my behalf.

That's what weakness makes us do: weakness makes us stop.

Weakness forces us into waiting—waiting for something bigger than we are to fix what is broken, to right what is wrong.

Every doctor's office I've been to has a waiting room. We will sit there, sometimes for hours, to see the doctor—usually because we don't have any other choice. We need what the doctor can offer us, and we will sit around and read old magazines and stare at the ceiling until we get in.

The road of weakness, it turns out, leads us straight into waiting. It's a painful place to be. It's one we'd never choose on our own.

Where Waiting Leads Us

On days when my weakness is most pronounced, I often wonder where God is. It's not that I wonder where he is on a map. And I don't wonder if God is with me—I know, from the Scriptures and from that moment in the wood-paneled hallway, that he has never left me, never forsaken me. I know that somehow, spiritually and physically, he is with me, inhabiting me through the Holy Spirit. I know that he is present, that he is here and everywhere. But sometimes there is a disconnect between my cognitive knowledge of God's goodness and strength, and my experiential reality. There are times when I can't *feel* his goodness and strength—often when I'm feeling my own weakness instead. And it has made me wonder where God is in weakness.

As a junior higher, I didn't understand how trich could be any good in my life—it seemed to bring only pain, and it felt like something that was directly opposed to God's Kingdom. Why wouldn't he just get rid of it for me? I started to see the other pains around me too: a family friend suffered from debilitating depression that refused to lift; why didn't God heal him? My grandmother was killed in a car crash when I was three years old; her absence in our family was real and difficult, and I didn't know how to reconcile that with my growing understanding of God as a good Father.

And yet I knew that God wasn't the source of evil and pain. He is not tempted by evil, nor does he tempt anyone into evil (see James 1:13). He came to save us from sin and evil and destruction. He is the one who will wipe away every tear (see Revelation 21:4). He is not and can never be the source of evil.

But God, it seems, does not equate evil with weakness in the same way I did—and, to be honest, the way I still do. I still look at weakness and wince. I take medicine or work harder or try again. I don't want to give in to weakness, because I don't like feeling weak.

And yet God seems to embrace weakness—value it, even. In fact, in Jesus we see the valuing of our frailty—of our flesh—with heavenly fervor. He became human. He didn't step into our flesh the way someone puts on a business suit, as something he could take off at the end of the day. Instead, the God of the universe, the one who holds stars like coins in his hand, the one who gives color to the northern lights, the one who knows the grooves of every tree, became *embodied*. He became human, and like us with our bones that break under too much pressure and our flesh that is so easily punctured, he knew weakness. He knew hunger and thirst (see Matthew 4:1-4), perhaps one of the ultimate signs of our weakness and dependence on things outside our control. And he did not despise our flesh.

Rather than seeing our weakness as something to avoid or get around, Jesus *entered into it*. When I look at weakness, I see only that weakness slows me down, holds me back, forces me to look into that cavern between who I am and who I want to be. And as a girl in junior high, I saw the weakness of trich as something that kept me from what I desired—normalcy, beauty, freedom.

That's not how God looks at weakness. Because God, remember, doesn't equate weakness with evil. It was hard for me to grasp this reality in my youth; it's still hard for me to grasp as an adult.

The apostle Paul famously declared that he would boast in his weakness. This passage from 2 Corinthians is mind boggling to me; it runs against everything I'm used to aiming for—strength, wholeness, ability. Paul said he prayed three times that God would take away his "thorn in the flesh"—he writes it as if three times is a great deal. Now maybe that's because Paul was amazingly holy and he prayed each time for ten days while fasting. Regardless, the response he received from God is what turned his pleading into boasting. God told Paul, "My grace is sufficient for you, for my power is made perfect in weakness" (2 Corinthians 12:9). From that place of hearing God's response to his suffering, Paul says he's able to "delight in weaknesses," for "when I am weak, then I am strong" (2 Corinthians 12:10, NIV).

The Greek word for weakness in this passage is *astheneia*. It can refer to a weakness of the body or the soul, but both types are connected to a lack of strength. The precise definition is "want of strength."[4] This weakness in the body can be due to frailty or illness, while the weakness of the soul is the inability—the lack of strength—to understand something, to restrain ourselves from doing something wrong, to carry burdens and trials, or to do anything glorious or great.[5]

So when Paul boasts about his weakness here, he is boasting about his lack of strength, his physical frailty, and his inability to do anything wonderful on his own. And it seems that Paul accepted his own weakness because he experienced God's unending strength when he found himself in lack—literally "in want"—of his own strength.

In my struggle with the weakness of trich, I couldn't see any of that. I still wanted my own strength. I wanted a body that always functioned well, a brain that didn't skip and stutter and resort to pulling out brows and lashes. I wanted to be done with trichotillomania. But maybe I was missing what God was telling me.

Did I believe that trich was from him, that he forced it on me or gave it to me? No. He is a good Father, incapable of giving anything but a good gift. Trich was part of the brokenness of our world. Yet as I ponder these passages now, I wonder if I was unable—or unwilling—to hear what God wanted me to know in those years. God is not deaf (see Isaiah 59:1). He was not ignoring me. He heard every single one of my prayers. Did I have ears, then, to hear what he wanted to say to me?

Could I have accepted it if he told me that my weakness didn't disgust or repel him in the same way my weakness disgusted me? Could I have heard it if he asked me to enter into my weakness rather than run away from it? Could I have received it if he was telling me that the strength I can access through him is greater than any strength I have in myself?

Maybe he was trying to tell me, as I leaned over that cavern of my own weakness and gazed at where I wanted to stand on the other side, that he was not only the bridge but the other side itself. Maybe what I was yearning for so much in wanting to be strong was not actually the ability to stop pulling out my own eyelashes. Maybe what I was yearning for so much was him.

It was both, of course. I wanted freedom from the condition, and I wanted Jesus. At times though, I think my desire for freedom from trich eclipsed my desire for Jesus. I wanted my own strength more than I wanted him.

And that's what needed to die in me. There was a choice before me, it seemed, even as young as I was. I couldn't have articulated it this way at the time, but it was the choice between my own strength and the strength of Christ. What I was just starting to learn was that I probably couldn't have both. From what Paul says, the way to experience Christ's strength is to not only acknowledge my weakness but boast in it. *Boast.* If that meant embracing and accepting my weakness rather than ramrodding against it every day, I had much to learn. I still do.

I am still learning that my weakness is a pathway to Jesus. That the ways I fail and the ways I don't measure up actually act as a vehicle to meeting Jesus in my daily life.

This is what threads throughout the Gospels, isn't it? Jesus encountering people in their brokenness and, in their places of weakness, revealing his ability to fill the cavern between who they are and who they want to be. Consider the blind men on the road who cried out to Jesus for healing. It was their blindness that offered them a reason to need Jesus tangibly (see Matthew 20:29-34). What about the woman stooped over at the synagogue? It was her weakness that drew Jesus' attention and led to her healing and glorification of God (see Luke 13:10-17). And the Bleeding Woman, who was desperate for healing, encountered Jesus because she needed a touch from someone greater than herself. Ultimately, it was her weakness that led her to him. Weakness points us to our need for a Savior.

This is what Paul was saying, I think—what he was getting at in this passage about prayer and weakness and boasting. He knew that his weakness was what revealed his need for God and that neediness is our truest condition: we are a people in need of God. If our weaknesses act as the gateway for us to see our own need, they become gifts. If trichotillomania helped me acknowledge my daily, hourly need for God's nearness and love, then it could become a gift to me. It could become a place where I could boast in who God is, rather than attempting to muscle through something yet again.

I wasn't there yet, in my junior high years. I wasn't at that place of boasting. I still had the deep-seated tendency to want to press past my weakness.

If I'm being honest, I still have that tendency. I am not yet like Paul; my knee-jerk reaction is to try to avoid weakness. The world swirling around us encourages us to sidestep weakness in any way we can. But I am learning that as I live in weakness—headaches, relational hurts, sickness, sorrow, whatever that weakness may be—I am living in waiting.

I am still waiting for healing, still waiting for wholeness in many areas of my life. I imagine that you are too. Whether it's a broken body, a broken relationship, a broken heart, or a broken mind—we are all waiting in our weakness for someone bigger than we are to step in and help us.

But just as God doesn't equate evil with weakness, he doesn't equate waiting with evil either. The weaknesses that force us—perhaps it would be better to say that *lead* us—into waiting aren't bad things. The weakness—the sickness or the grief or the financial tenuousness—may not have come from God, who does not create evil. But he can allow those weaknesses to lead us into a place of waiting where we are solely dependent upon him.

And that is a gift. The gift of weakness is that it leads us to the only strong one. And his strength is enough. Enough for this day. Enough for this life.

More than enough, actually. It is all that we need.

CHAPTER 3

When Waiting Costs You Everything

As the years piled up, the doctor's visits had piled up too, like dust in an unswept corner. Sarah's father had approached her four years into it all, with tears at the corners of his aging eyes. "The doctor's visits will have to be paid for out of your dowry now." His voice was barely more than a whisper. She nodded quickly, wanting him to turn away, pained by the twist of his face.

Sarah knew she was the cause of his sorrow. How much had she disappointed him? How much had she taken from him without ever giving him anything back? He had reached out to put his hand on her shoulder, but Sarah had already turned away to knead more bread, the role she had taken over from her mother years ago. Both Sarah and her father had left the short conversation crying, neither one knowing the other's tears.

Before it even seemed possible, her entire dowry had been spent on doctors. Two hundred denarii—all of it, poured out like water on dry earth.[1] *Every linen robe and piece of jewelry that her mother had set aside for her had been sold. Even the earrings set with lapis lazuli that she loved so dearly, the ones she had hoped to wear on her wedding day, were gone.*

Sarah kept waiting to wake up and be done with her bleeding; in her dreams, she lived her life before the blood came, before she had become a burden and a liability. But when morning broke, she woke to days filled with increasing sorrow—and no healing in sight. She was still unclean; she had memorized the law that declared her fate. A thousand times over, she had searched it through, mulling it over in her mind for a way to get around the rules that God had decreed:

When a woman has a discharge, and the discharge in her body is blood, she shall be in her menstrual impurity for seven days, and whoever touches her shall be unclean until the evening. And everything on which she lies during her menstrual impurity shall be unclean. Everything also on which she sits shall be unclean. And whoever touches her bed shall wash his clothes and bathe himself in water and be unclean until the evening. And whoever touches anything on which she sits shall wash his clothes and bathe himself in water and be unclean until the evening. Whether it is the bed or anything on which she sits, when he touches it he shall be unclean until the evening. And if any man lies with her and her menstrual impurity comes upon him, he shall be unclean seven days, and every bed on which he lies shall be unclean.

If a woman has a discharge of blood for many days, not at the time of her menstrual impurity, or if she has a discharge beyond the time of her impurity, all the days of the discharge she shall continue in uncleanness. As in the days of her impurity, she shall be unclean.

LEVITICUS 15:19-25

I am that woman, *Sarah thought. I am the woman who has bled for many days. I am the woman who is always unclean.*

Had there ever been another woman like her? She had never heard of someone who bled like her, not even for a day or two more past the seven in every month.

That was why the money had to be spent, of course: until she stopped bleeding and was ceremonially clean according to the law, she could never marry, she could never attend worship, and she could hardly leave her house, lest she make everyone she touched unclean.

And now there was no money left and nothing to be done. Her mother had traveled with her to other villages, other cities. They even went to Jerusalem to meet with a well-known doctor there. But nothing worked. She had spent all she had, and still—still—she bled.

All that she had, gone. All that she had hoped for, gone. Sarah knew it: she had nothing left.

47

For the most part, I loved high school. I know, I know—crazy, right? But I thrived. It was a small high school. I was an athlete, I had good friends, and I loved classes so much that I usually didn't mind the homework. I'm a nerd at heart—it's part of why I would later pursue academia and writing—and I was happy in my nerdiness; happy in the classroom; happy with my studies, my sports practices, and my friends.

But high school is also the time when girls, as a general rule, start to wear makeup; it's when looks really start to matter in social standing; it's when boys and dates and dances and appearances become increasingly important.

And my trich was getting worse. It was now obvious, unless I wore my carefully crafted regimen of makeup, that I didn't have normal eyebrows or lashes. It looked like I had gone haywire with my tweezers; often, I had just a thin line of brows that were more pencil than hair. My eyelashes were nearly gone most of the time too.

So I purchased false eyelashes at the drugstore, securing the most normal-looking pair of Ardell's full lashes I could find. I didn't want the dramatic ones, the feathery ones, or the extra-dark ones; I just wanted the pair that looked the most subtle and unobtrusive. I slipped them in with my mom's order on the conveyor belt every other week; she would rub my back and tell me she loved me, quietly acknowledging the battle I was always fighting. Later, when I got my license, I would drive to the store myself, look around to make sure no one I knew was in the checkout line, and buy a fresh pair when my current ones were wearing out.

I usually stuffed the white plastic bag in my purse and drove home to put on the new pair of fake lashes. Standing in front of the bathroom mirror, I gently unpeeled them from their case and held them lightly. If you've never held false lashes, they look like two waning moons—soft crescents in your hand.

And here's what you must do: first, you cut them down to the right length. You snip off the ends of the falsies, making them match the length of your lid line. Then you pick up one in your left hand, between your thumb and forefinger, making sure to grasp it carefully, while you hold the tiny tube of lash glue in your right. You need a steady hand to squirt a thin, even line of glue along the edge of the false lash. Then you have to wait three to five seconds for the glue to catch the air and start to harden. When it begins to mellow from bright white to mild yellow, you put the tube down and hold on to the falsie at each end—this part requires both hands. After that you try to force the tacky glue as close to your own lash line as possible, pushing down the minuscule edges and praying they will cling to the inner and outer corners of your upper eye. Those are the hardest places to get them to stick.

If the glue adheres, it will make your whole eyelid feel heavy and tired; you will probably want a nap, but your work has just begun. Because now you must try to make what is fake look normal. So you take your liquid eyeliner and draw a line under the false eyelashes, where your real eyelashes *should* be. It will take a thick, dark line to make it look like the fake lashes are even possibly real. You will look like you are heading to the prom every day of your life.

But it's better than letting everyone see your real lash line, bare and ugly.

The High Price of Hiding

I wore those falsies most days in high school, but the problem with wearing false eyelashes is that they don't stay on when they come into contact with water. That meant tears, pools, lakes, and sweating were all bad news. So water was off limits for me, unless I wanted the adhesive glue to shrink back from my eyelids and curl up, leaving me with little caterpillars of black fringe crawling along my lash line.

For years, that meant that I avoided most things that involved water. Pool parties were a definite no—or if I went, I "forgot" my suit and hung out on the ledge. Any tear-jerking movie was suspect, as was poetry by Pablo Neruda.

I couldn't avoid this problem entirely, though: I was a crier. I still am. I cry easily and often.

Also, I was an athlete, and I loved playing volleyball too much to give it up, even though sweating was a definite no-no with fake lashes.

And let's be honest: my sweat game is *strong*. I have never been a girl who "glows" while working out. I don't shine or shimmer in the gym. My cheeks don't get that slightly flushed look. I am more of the red-faced, soak-through-your-T-shirt variety of athlete. If it's true that sweat is fat crying, then my body was *weeping* every day at volleyball practice. Absolutely *sobbing*. So you can imagine why I couldn't wear my fake eyelashes on the court—there was simply too much sweat, every practice, every game.

I was too embarrassed to tell any of my teammates about trichotillomania. I didn't want them to think I was weird or strange or sick. So every day during volleyball season, I would head to the locker room after class and choose a bathroom stall. There, I sat on the toilet and peeled off the falsies, placing them in a little pillbox I carried with me just for that purpose. With a small mirror in one hand and my mascara in the other, I tried to create some semblance of normalcy with my eyes. I never went anywhere without those two items—my mirror and my mascara—not because I was vain, but because I was scared. I prayed no one would look at me too closely as we were running drills and plays.

I don't know if my teammates noticed or not. If they did, they never said anything.

Looking back now, it breaks my heart that I carried such fear for so long, and I have deep compassion for my high school self. I was so afraid of someone finding out that I had trich, of being seen as different or broken or weak. I think, in part, it was because I was successful in so many other areas that I didn't want to break the image I hoped others had of me. Honestly, I think I didn't want to break the image I had of myself. I couldn't untangle the lie from the truth: I thought that *any* brokenness would taint the successes in my life. I couldn't see that my daily failures with trich didn't define me or negate my strengths.

So I hid my struggle, even from the friends who knew me best.

But at what cost? In my young life, the cost was huge. Hiding trichotillomania from my friends and teammates cost me a great deal—in time and in energy and in friendship.

In time: I spent more hours in front of the mirror than I care to remember, fixing and refixing those false eyelashes, trying to redraw my browline, trying to hide this condition that kept growing worse.

In energy: I relinquished massive amounts of emotional and mental energy trying to hide my condition, trying to avoid situations that would reveal my condition, trying to think of other ways I might be able to appear normal (sunglasses, hats to cover my eyebrows—anything).

In friendship: What I didn't know then was that friendship is built on the back of brokenness and that intimacy with others often stems from shared pain. I knew that my family was a safe place, that they loved me even in my weakness. But I didn't trust that my peers could love me in my brokenness too. I kept friends at an arm's length in the one area of my life where I desperately needed communion. I wanted to hold on to my self-protection more than I wanted deep friendship.

When You Run Out of Options

The cost I paid in my high school years for struggling with trich was mostly emotional and relational. But I can assure you: I would have paid any price to be free of trichotillomania. And for me, that's saying a lot. Although I hope I've grown into a more generous and gracious woman, I was cautious with my stuff as a teenager. It was harder than I'd like to admit for me to part with money when I was in high school. I'm not quite sure why; my parents were financially stable and unendingly generous with my sister and me. But it always felt like security to me to have money in the bank, even if my own money amounted to very little in the world's eyes. I wanted to have something to my name. *Just in case things didn't work out.*

Careful as I was with the little money I had in high school, I know that if there had been a way for me to be rid of trichotillomania, I would have spent my entire savings without thinking twice. It would have felt like nothing to give up all the money I had in the bank for a legitimate shot at being fully and completely healed. My parents did this in their own way, spending what they could to try to help me be free from trich: money for books to learn about my condition, money for herbal supplements that some doctors thought might work, money for behavioral modification counseling. They wanted to help me, and they would have spent every penny to our family's name if someone had offered the hope of a cure.

That's precisely what the Bleeding Woman did. She spent all she had, stretching out her hands in the hope that someone—anyone—might finally have the remedy she'd been searching for. I imagine her bartering her jewelry for medicines that did no good. I imagine her knowing that she was down to her last stack of coins but handing them over to the doctor anyway, hoping against hope that she might finally be healed and start her life afresh.

The Bleeding Woman was willing to spend it all because she had no other choice—no future ahead of her. As extreme as it sounds, I don't think it was folly for her to fling all of her coins at the chance of wholeness. Healing was what she desired most of all, more than anything. So it makes sense that all her earthly wealth went toward trying to secure that healing.

When it comes down to it, most of us are willing to spend our money on whatever we value most. For the Bleeding Woman, it was healing. She valued healing above any amount of money. For the merchant in the parable, it was the pearl of great price. He sold all he had on one pearl of "great value" (see Matthew 13:45-46).

Yes, we spend ourselves on what we value the most. Whether it's money, time, energy, or emotions, we pour ourselves out on the thing that we deem most worthy of our devotion.

When I was in high school, I spent myself on hiding. I spent my time and energy and emotions on concealing trich—on trying to keep up appearances. That was what cost me dearly, the thing I was unwilling to part with. I refused to let go of my desire to keep up appearances. I paid for that desire every day, when I looked in the mirror and when I was negotiating falsies in the locker room stall. I paid for it in every conversation I needed to have with friends but didn't.

At the heart of it all, the cost of what we are devoted to is never really about money or time or energy. It's about what's behind the price we pay; it's about the desperation we feel to secure what we want. For the Bleeding Woman, spending all her money on doctors was about her desperation to be healed and whole. For me, the cost of my time and energy was about my desperation to keep up the appearance of normalcy.

And ultimately, when we put our desperation in anything other than God himself, those things become idols. We can never pay enough; eventually, they let us down. The Bleeding Woman spent all she had on doctors but only grew worse. I spent my time and energy keeping up appearances, but it didn't work—at least never for very long.

As hard as I tried to keep my eyelashes looking normal by wearing falsies almost every day, there were times when I was just plain tired, when I didn't want to deal with the ten- or twenty-minute ordeal of positioning the fake lashes *just so*. And that's why, occasionally, when I didn't think my trich was too bad, I would go out with friends sans lashes, wearing only mascara and eyeliner.

It was at a basketball game that I got called out. A group of us had made the drive across town to see our high school team try to beat one of the other Corn Belt Conference squads.

We filled in two rows on the bleachers. I was sitting in the lower row, which meant a few of my friends were sitting above me. During one of the time-outs, Jane leaned down and tapped my shoulder.

"Ann, what happened to your eyelashes? They're, like, almost gone!"

I gasped.

I wanted to run away or disappear. Me, the girl who loved attention and loved making new friends. Me, the girl on the starting volleyball team, the one who loved raising her hand in class and singing loud in the choir. That's not the girl I was in the bleachers that night. In that moment, I wavered between sobbing and fleeing. I felt small and humiliated.

Jane's question hung in the air. But how do you speak of a struggle you've been hiding from the day it began? How do you casually chat about it in the middle of a high school basketball game? And how do you keep from falling apart when someone finally asks the question you've feared most?

I had no idea what to say.

So I lied.

"What do you mean? It's just how they grow." I stood up, midplay. "I'm gonna go find the bathroom."

I ran to the bathroom farthest away from the court and the noise and my friends and stood at the mirror to examine myself. In front of a row of deserted sinks, I looked at myself square in the face, trying to see what Jane saw.

I looked tired. At seventeen, I had the eyelashes and eyebrows of an old woman, with lashes that were short, spiky, and sticking out in odd directions. My makeup was heavy; I was trying to hide everything with liner and the darkest mascara I could find. Like everything else with trich, it wasn't working.

I could have cried, but I knew it would only ruin my makeup. So I swallowed my belly of tears, gulped a deep breath and then another one, and let my feet walk me back to the game. If I was gone too long, I knew Jane would only ask more questions, and I couldn't handle any more questions that night.

When I got back to the bleachers, I made sure to sit on a row above my friends. I didn't say much; I just clapped at the appropriate times. My heart was a thousand miles away, hiding.

The Down Payment of Surrender

There is a desperation that comes when we need something from God—when we feel like we are frantic for something from his hand—and we will often part with anything of value to get what we want. The Bleeding Woman wanted healing, and she gave up everything in an attempt to get it.

That impulse hasn't changed in the two thousand years since. A friend of mine whose son has been diagnosed with cancer at the age of two would pay any amount to ensure his health and life. Another friend has spent thousands upon thousands of dollars on IVF in order to conceive a child.

To varying degrees, we all give up time and energy and emotional wholeness—and sometimes money—to cover up the places that feel the weakest in our lives. We wear different clothes to hide the pounds we've gained, we elude conversations that may be painful, we avoid people who have hurt us, we stop trying to make new friends, we stop going to church, we stop praying, we stop hoping. Our lives feel hollowed out, painful to the touch.

Because while desperation has its own cost, there's another cost most of us face in those painful places. It's the cost of waiting.

When we have to wait for God to move on our behalf—when we find ourselves at the end of whatever rope we're hugging—it's painful.

That's because waiting demands that we pay.

Waiting demands that we pay, because when we are forced to wait for God's work—for his healing, for his provision, for his answer—the waiting itself becomes a high cost. We come to a point in waiting for his breakthrough when it feels like too much to bear. The waiting is the thing that hurts—sometimes even more than the initial pain we faced.

For those who have walked through infertility for years, the waiting becomes, perhaps, their biggest cost. Their days are scarred by the seeming silence of God, by what feels like unanswered prayers, by the years winding and winding toward—what? Where? There is no end in sight, just more waiting.

For those who want to be married but have no prospects in sight, the waiting can feel like a burden, like an endless sea they can never swim far enough to cross. As they face the pain of a lack of options, of watching others find a spouse and have children, of feeling like the heavens have shuttered their dreams, the waiting is hurtful, even overwhelming.

For those who feel stuck in their jobs, their lives, their marriages—those who desperately want a change but don't know where to go or what to do—the waiting wears them down like sandpaper on wood. As they are confronted with a lack of vision, a lack of hope, a lack of clarity from the God they follow, they struggle in the waiting.

Waiting is hard. Especially when there's no apparent end in sight.

It was in high school that the waiting with trich started to wear on me. In every other area of my life, I was able to pay the cost required when things felt hard or challenging. I got a tutor when I needed to pass math class. I lived on little sleep when I had big tests or assignments due. And in volleyball, when I developed a hairline fracture in my left foot, I played anyway. I played when the pain became acute, the bones threatening to separate and loosen like a wishbone being pulled apart after a Thanksgiving meal. I played when the doctor (and the X-ray) told me it was time to rest and let my body heal. I played because I was willing to pay—in pain—for the opportunity to win the state championship with my team.

But five and six and seven years into having trichotillomania, I found I couldn't pay the cost for getting rid of trich, because there was no cost left to pay. Time? Check. Energy? Check. Professional counseling? Check. Behavior modification? Check. Prayer? Check.

No cost was enough.

At the intersection of my ache for healing and my inability to be healed, I started to encounter a deep soul weariness that I would carry with me for a long time. I had hoped that I would grow out of trichotillomania or that I would finally be able to will myself to stop, but by eighteen, I had an internal knowing that trich was never going to just go away. I came to understand that this weakness would be my companion until God healed me. I knew this with such certainty because I had nothing left to pay. There was nothing else I could give to try to make myself better.

This wasn't a realization I wanted to make, but as I wrote papers and took exams and visited colleges and applied for scholarships, I came to terms with the fact that I was going to be waiting for healing from trichotillomania until God healed me.

I would sit at the family computer keyboard, trying to

type a paper but pulling out my lashes instead. The white keyboard would end up covered in black lashes while I argued against my tears and self-disgust. I would blow on the keyboard, scattering the lashes onto the desk and then to the floor, trying to forget what I couldn't stop doing to my own body.

I wasn't going to be able to heal myself.

This wasn't a momentary realization but a growing sense of helplessness. After years marked by the accumulation of pages littered with lashes, of keyboards hiding lashes in their creases, of textbooks with eyelashes stuck in the spine, I began to acknowledge my soul's disappointment and my heart's pain. Without one single week free from trichotillomania for seven years, I felt defeated. I was desperate for God to heal me.

The waiting sheared down my strength and hope. That's because there's a cost to waiting that's impossible to ignore: the cost of self-sufficiency. Waiting forces us to surrender our reliance on our own ability to pay up, to come through, to make it happen.

The cost of waiting demands the payment of our self-sufficiency, and we pay in our acknowledgment of our inability to be enough.

The Gift of Insufficiency

The Bleeding Woman felt the cost of waiting too. The price of her own self-sufficiency must have been painfully evident to her after twelve years of bleeding. She'd spent it all—every denarius she had was gone, spent on midwives and doctor bills and remedies that did nothing for her. Her dowry had likely been lost over the years, and with it her hope of marriage. It wasn't just the money she was losing—it was her entire dream for a future. She was desperate enough to let her money dwindle to nothing as she looked for a cure, and in the process, she was forced to part with her own self-sufficiency. Now she had no money and therefore no ability to be self-reliant even if she wished to be.

The cost of waiting is the paring down of our illusion of self-sufficiency. That moment at the basketball game when Jane asked me about my lashes megaphoned the message to my tender heart: I couldn't do it. I couldn't keep up the facade. Hard as I tried, I was still failing—both because I was pulling out my own eyelashes and because I couldn't cover it up.

Busted.

But that's the truth of it, isn't it? We are never really self-sufficient. We can never create enough resources, enough wisdom, enough health. So waiting often means that we experience the cost of seeing ourselves *as we actually are*—broken, weak, and unable to fix our lives. It is a high cost, a painful one. But it's a cost that must be paid, and it's a cost we have to pay if we are to walk in step with Jesus.

This is not theoretical for me; I have lived out the cost of my own inadequacy. Trich pushed me, time and time again, to the place of awareness—and acknowledgment—of my complete lack of self-sufficiency. Just when I was doing well in school or got asked to the prom, or even when our team won the state championship, I would fall back into pulling out my own eyelashes—a compulsive, continual reminder of my inability to live the life I wanted to live.

We all wrestle with this inability, in one way or another. My friend Michelle struggles with depression—she wants to feel joyful and content but can't will herself into that place. My friend Charlotte has gained twenty pounds in the last several years and can't seem to get to a weight where she feels comfortable in her own skin. Some dear friends have been trying to adopt for a long time, but nothing is moving in the governmental process. All of us keep ramming into these walls that remind us of how much we can't do, how powerless we are to muscle through.

And yet this awareness of our own insufficiency is, itself, a gift.

I know; it never feels like a gift. In the moment, it feels like pain. When I was in high school, my inability to free myself from trich seemed like an unwelcome gift I never wanted to unwrap; it felt like the sting of rejection, like the ache of hollow promises.

I didn't want to have trichotillomania. I wanted to be done with it. But when I came to terms with the fact that I couldn't heal myself, that was the place where I encountered Jesus.

We had a special service at my church just for high schoolers, and the gym was full of two or three hundred teenagers every Sunday, worshiping Jesus. I loved that church, loved the electric feeling of singing next to friends from school who were also learning to love Jesus and follow him. I loved the fact that the adults there treated us like adults too. They preached the Bible to us as if we were able to understand and comprehend the truth of the Scripture, and it made me want to understand more. I grew thirsty for truth.

One Sunday we had a special speaker who was talking about purity and honoring God with our bodies: "Do you not know that your body is a temple of the Holy Spirit within you, whom you have from God? You are not your own, for you were bought with a price. So glorify God in your body" (1 Corinthians 6:19-20).

And while I knew that the speaker was talking about sexual purity and dating, for me that verse pointed to something else. My body—it wasn't mine. Jesus had already paid the highest price for it. He made the ultimate sacrifice for my body—even for my eyelashes, even for trich. He knew—through a thousand prayers, he knew—how much I loathed this condition, how much I longed to be rid of it. He knew that I wanted to stop pulling out my own lashes but couldn't accomplish it on my own. He understood all that was in my heart.

And so, accepting that Jesus had already purchased my body, just as it was, I gave up the franticness I had been clinging to—that panicky need to get rid of trichotillomania. I knew I would still try to stop pulling, would still try to look normal. My desire to be healed had not changed. But I laid down any false thought that I had the ability to fix myself.

I would wait.

It was all I could do. Wait on Jesus.

Waiting Well

Alone, none of us can overcome our weaknesses, stop our sins, obtain healing, or find happiness. Our attempts to control our own destinies prove futile. Love crumbles, we lose our jobs, we experience a miscarriage, healing doesn't come. If we stop long enough, we become unmistakably aware of our inability to pay the cost for the things we so deeply desire. Waiting only makes that awareness more acute; it forces us to stop long enough to notice all that we aren't attaining, all that we aren't getting.

And that's why, as we wait for God's breakthrough in our lives, it will cost us a great deal. In fact, waiting well—waiting rightly—will cost us all that we have. It will cost us our illusion of control. It will cost us our self-sufficiency. It will mean coming to terms with our inability to make anything happen—and it will mean tossing ourselves at the feet of Jesus and asking him to do what we cannot.

But there we will discover that the gift of waiting is that *in the waiting*—in what may even feel like languishing—we can encounter Jesus.

Jesus, the great cost-payer. Jesus, the one who paid the highest price of all time for all our brokenness—the price of his own life and blood:

> You were ransomed from the futile ways inherited
> from your forefathers, not with perishable things
> such as silver or gold, but with the precious blood of
> Christ, like that of a lamb without blemish or spot.
> He was foreknown before the foundation of the

world but was made manifest in the last times for the
sake of you who through him are believers in God,
who raised him from the dead and gave him glory,
so that your faith and hope are in God.

I PETER 1:18-21

Jesus alone knows the true cost of brokenness and sin,
the true cost of weakness and failure: he has already paid
for it on the cross. So we can trust him. We can trust that
as we struggle with sickness or disease, as we struggle with a
broken marriage or a disobedient child, as we struggle with
our sorrows and our sin and our own wayward hearts, he
understands. He has already paid the cost. That is why, as
we wait for him to do what we cannot—to heal us, to help
us, to make a way where there is no way—we can trust him.

Our God is the one who did not withhold even his own
Son for us (see Romans 8:32). He is the one who was willing
to pay the highest cost for us. He will give us what we need,
even if it is not in our way or our timing.

And until that day, we wait.

CHAPTER 4

When Waiting
Claims Your Identity

By the time Sarah was nineteen, the town knew why she would not marry. Somehow the secret had slipped out—that she was bleeding unendingly—and the assumptions of those in her village proved true. She was defective, unclean, unable to marry. It would have been impossible to hide for much longer, Sarah told herself. Her inability to participate in any Temple worship or community celebrations was easier to hide when she was a child. Now that she was clearly a woman, her absence at worship and festivals was becoming obvious. She wanted to go, wanted to participate in community life. But she could not. The law kept her away from any sense of normal life. Far, far away.

And so her life was simple and small: she spent most days within the walls of her home, trying to contribute to the family life in

*whatever way she could. Her sister was married now, and pregnant.
Her older brothers worked outside the home, caring for families of
their own. Her younger brother was apprenticed to a carpenter.
Sarah kneaded and kneaded and kneaded bread. She swept every
day, and she tended the tree whose roots were beginning to threaten
the foundation of the house. But she did not go to market, and she
did not go to worship, and she did not go out for weddings or festivals or celebrations.*

*None of the broths she drank or the cures she tried ever stopped
the bleeding. She tried fasting, tried wine mixed with alum, tried
everything that was required of her. She even offered extra sacrifices,
although her parents did not know about it. While she could not go
to the Temple herself, she asked her brother to take small pigeons to
the priests on her behalf so the holy men could make atonement for
a sin she wondered if she had committed but did not know about.*

*Yet still, she grew worse. The bleeding was heavier now than it
had ever been. And she started to name herself by what she knew she
was: a bleeder. It was the only way she could see herself anymore—
as the Bleeding Woman. All other markers of who she wanted to be,
of who she could have been, had been swept away in the years of
blood. A bleeder: it was the only identity she had left.*

There are many ways I have identified myself over the years.
"Tall" is one identifier; "sensitive" is another. "Conscientious"
is one that most of my teachers used, which is a nice way of
saying that I was kind of obsessed about homework and getting things right.

One identifier I have always desired is "beautiful." As a little girl, I dressed up as a princess before I put on my sneakers and went to tennis lessons. A few years later, I wore my mother's heels around the house, even though they were several sizes too large, and then traded her heels for my basketball shoes. As much as I loved athletic shorts and ponytails, I enjoyed being girly and always wanted to be beautiful. I haven't yet met a woman who doesn't care about being beautiful, at least on some level. The versions and ideals of beauty differ for each person, but even those who rebel against the cultural standards of beauty are often aiming for some expression of uniqueness—for their own definition of what it means to be beautiful.

The thing about trichotillomania—part of the reason I had such a hard time embracing my weakness—was the way it slithered into my identity, especially during my late high school years and into college. Being someone who pulled out my own eyelashes shaped my identity. It was an identity I loathed, but it was one I knew comfortably.

To someone who isn't a trichotillomaniac, it's hard to explain how zealously I thought about eyelashes. It's telling, what you notice when you're obsessed with something. As someone who tugged on my lashes and brows, I saw eyelashes *everywhere*. Every magazine bulged with ads for "longer, thicker lashes"; TV commercials and billboards portrayed images of women with fluttering lashes that exuded femininity and appeal. The constant reminder hovered over me, highlighting that I didn't even have the lashes needed to carry the mascara they were advertising. Never mind having "lashes to infinity" or "4x the lash fullness." I just wanted to have a regular spread of lashes on my eyelids.

Eyelashes appear to be the stunning facial accessory that everyone has—and that no one can seem to get enough of. Women's eyes in particular have been a cultural obsession for thousands of years. Early makeup was most likely applied as part of religious rituals but later became associated with beauty and adornment in ancient cultures. Egyptian, Roman, Greek, and Japanese women—all of them found their own type of remedy for lackluster eyes. Kohl, plant-based substances, and even bird droppings were used to darken the lids and lashes. For centuries, various cultures have had their own ways of securing applied beauty.

And I had mine. I never left the house without makeup on. It was like putting on my glasses or pants: makeup was not optional. I was simply too embarrassed to go anywhere without my false eyelashes on, or at least mascara. There were mornings in college, blurry from late-night study sessions the evening before, when I would throw on a dirty pair of jeans and the closest sweatshirt I could find, and then spend fifteen minutes preparing my lashes before leaving the dorm room. Even partially hidden behind glasses, I was still afraid that someone would see me without makeup.

But living in a dorm my freshman year meant that I was assigned a roommate. Her name was Jessica, and on move-in day, I remember seeing her down the long hallway of our dorm floor for the first time. We both squealed and ran toward each other, and our friendship was born in a mash of tears and hugs (she was an easy crier too). This was in the days before social media ran the world. We had talked on the phone maybe once or twice before the semester started, and we knew hardly anything about each other. All we knew was that we were both on the college volleyball team and that we would be roommates. But once I met Jess in person, I knew so much more: I knew we were going to be best friends.

Friendship with Jess came easily; she was easygoing where I was uptight, and quick to laugh where I was quick to worry. She was fast to forgive when I was nervous if she would. We were instantaneous friends. Looking back, I see that she was much easier to live with than I was. She was clean and quiet and went to bed early (I . . . was none of those things). But she loved me for who I was and never made me feel like I had to change. Outside my own family, I had never known a friend like this—one who simply loved me and enjoyed me in all my quirkiness.

We lived in a dorm with a communal bathroom, which meant that Jess saw pretty much everything about me really quickly, whether she wanted to or not. I realized—fast—that I wasn't going to be able to hide my false eyelashes from her. I wasn't going to apply them in front of the huge mirror in the bathroom shared by thirty other women. Either I'd have to wake up ridiculously early to apply them before everyone else was awake or I'd have to tell Jess why I was putting on fake eyelashes in our room.

If you knew me, you'd know that getting up early wasn't really an option. It's like asking me to fly: a girl can dream, but the dream always comes crashing down.

And so, pretty quickly in that first semester of freshman

year, I told Jess about trich. I knew that I had to, and although I was scared, there was also part of me that deeply wanted to tell her.

One day we were in our dorm room hanging out. It was just the two of us.

"Jess?"

"Mm-hmm?" She was working on her computer, and the room was filled with the soft *tap-tap* of her fingers thwacking the keyboard.

"I want to tell you something."

I don't know if it was my tone or the trembling in my voice, but Jessica turned around in her chair and gave me her full attention.

I started crying.

"Ann? Are you okay?" Effortlessly maternal, Jess rushed over to sit next to me on the couch. She put her hand on my back. "What's the matter?"

I tried to take a deep breath. "I know this probably isn't going to make any sense, but I want to tell you about this condition that I have."

She nodded and started rubbing my back in large, looping circles.

"For about eight years, I've been pulling out my own eyelashes and eyebrows. It's called trichotillomania." Everything came tumbling out. "I can't stop it. I want to, and I hate that I deal with this, but I wanted you to know." I couldn't stop the tears from coming; my cheeks were soaked with them. "It makes me really embarrassed and ashamed, and I'm afraid you're going to think I'm weird."

Jessica looked at me, her own eyes wet. Her voice was quiet. "Ann, I don't think you're weird." She paused. "You don't have anything to be ashamed of. We all have stuff we deal with." She gave me a hug, and I cried into her shoulder for a long time. I remember feeling relieved, and also as emotionally naked as I had ever been.

Maybe it sounds dramatic. Maybe it sounds like I was too intense about trich, like I cared too much. But after all the years of hiding this condition, after all the attempts to cover up what I'd struggled with for so long, everything came pitching into that moment as I sat on the blue couch in our dorm room. I had never opened this conversation before— I had never told anyone about my condition. My parents and sister and I talked about trich, but I hadn't needed to break it to them, to start the conversation. I was so young when trich started that it just became part of the fabric of our shared life and conversation; it was always there. When Jane asked about trich during the basketball game in high school, I had lied to avoid talking about it. But here, with Jess, I unwrapped the conversation because even though I was scared to tell her the truth, I was also ready. I didn't want to feel alone in this; I didn't want to live in hiding for another four years. I wanted to be free.

Jess was a wonderful grace to me. My fear of anyone finding out had come true—now she knew that I had this condition of trichotillomania. But she didn't treat me any differently; she didn't act like I was strange or fragile or odd. She wanted to know how she could help, so I told her, "If you see me starting to pull out an eyelash, just tell me." And she did. But other than that, Jess prayed for me, and she let me cry about it when I needed to.

To my surprise and relief, she didn't look at me through the lens of brokenness that I was so afraid of. Jess didn't judge me by my weakness. She didn't define me by my struggle.

Putting Your Best Face Forward

Even though Jess didn't view me through the lens of trich, I struggled to define myself any other way. For years, I'd defined myself as someone who pulled out her eyelashes. Yes, I thought of myself as a loving daughter, a fun sister, and a smart student. Yet when I thought about myself in terms of the large scale of my life, I saw someone who was mostly okay but had a looming red X in this one area. Essentially, I perceived myself as damaged—as someone with an unalterable flaw.

I understood the ridiculousness in this mentality when I actually spoke it out loud. Jess helped me start to see that. And as I took biblical theology classes as an undergraduate at Wheaton College, I started to intellectually understand that as a person of faith, as someone who has come to the cross and the empty tomb, I had already admitted that I was full of flaws, full of sin, full of brokenness. I didn't have a red X because of trich; my life *was* a red X apart from Jesus. As a Christian, I was confessing my inability to make it to God on my own. Because ultimately, to be a Christian means to acknowledge—and yes, accept—our deep brokenness.

Yet on a daily basis, I didn't think like this. I had head knowledge, but it wasn't yet trickling down to my heart or identity. Even though I acknowledged my need for salvation and my inability to be good and whole on my own, I still felt that cultural tug to be someone who had an identity to keep up and a face to put forward—in both the literal and allegorical senses of the word. I had unfastened the thought that I could heal myself, but I still wanted to be beautiful. Who doesn't?

So I still had a face to put forward: a face, in the sense of a facade that I presented to the world. *Facade*: rooted in French and pointing to the outer front of a building, one gilded or embellished to look lovely to a passerby. I don't necessarily mean that the face I presented to the world was false or insincere—I just knew that the side of me I offered to my professors or to the barista or to the lady in the lunch line wasn't all of me.

Just as the facade of an old building may be the only side adorned with embellishments and beautiful carvings, the facade I offered to the broader world was the purposefully presented side of me. I couldn't offer my internal struggles to my professor in intimate detail—it would have been both unhelpful and inappropriate. The lady in the lunch line didn't really need to—or care to—know about the personal struggles I was having that week (except for the struggle of the lost ID card, which is a sincere struggle if you have ever faced it). We all have places in our lives where facades are actually needed. We can't wear our hearts on our sleeves for everyone.

And I had an actual face that I presented to the world. With or without makeup, with or without false eyelashes, with or without a smile, it was the only face I had, and I wanted it to be beautiful. I had long ago given up any dream of being a model or a flawless beauty. But I wanted to be pretty in the ways I could be.

I didn't know how to bring the knowledge in my head—the awareness of my brokenness as a baseline reality and a starting point for my need for Jesus—in line with the emotions of my heart and my deep desire to feel whole and look beautiful.

I often wonder how the Bleeding Woman perceived herself. She hadn't always been the Bleeding Woman. In the early years of her life, perhaps for well over a decade, she hadn't been bleeding. She wasn't a bleeder. Then, at some point, she started bleeding and never stopped. I imagine that for the first week, the first ten days, even the first month, she assumed that her bleeding would end, that her life would return to normal. Maybe even for the first year, she was hopeful that she would be healed. But twelve years after she first bled, she certainly must have seen herself as a bleeder. By that point, the blood must have felt more normal than strange. I imagine her curling in bed in the dark, the blood still trickling even as her body tried to heal itself in the night. There in the shadows, maybe she tried to remember her life before the bleeding came. Had she ever been someone else?

The Gospel of Mark records these few lines about this woman's medical history: "There was a woman who had had a discharge of blood for twelve years, and who had suffered much under many physicians, and had spent all that she had, and was no better but rather grew worse" (Mark 5:25-26).

She had this unstoppable condition, and every doctor she saw only made her worse. One scholar records that the doctors "bungled" her care and that "all these years of human effort, not only afford[ed] no help" but "add[ed] to the patient's distress."[1] Like a tumor that defied all chemotherapy, like a broken bone that refused to set, her body would not stop bleeding. The doctors offered her what medicine they had: wine swirled with rubber alum, and then onions and crocuses.[2]

When that didn't work, I imagine the doctors offered her alternative therapies. Or perhaps they told her to stop thinking about her condition, to just believe it would go away. Perhaps the priests instructed her to make more sacrifices or offer better prayers. But still, nothing helped. And because she continued to bleed, she was, at least in religious terms, an outcast. According to Levitical law, she was unclean, shut out from religious life, and unable to enter fully into any Temple worship of Yahweh, the one with the unspeakable name, the one who could not be near anything impure.[3] And she *was* impure, consistently and without pause, for twelve years. All the time.

One scholar calls her existence "wretched" due to the fact that she was constantly unclean and would have been shunned by her community.[4] According to the law, if she touched another person, she would make that person unclean as well (see Leviticus 15:19-30). Another biblical scholar notes that she must have been filled with "despair over her loneliness and condition."[5] Think of it: a life with no hugs. A life with no touch. A life with no parties. A life of being shunned from her own people.

Longing for Normal

I became something of an expert at wearing false eyelashes. By the time I was in college, it was an art form I'd spent the better part of a decade perfecting, and although there were days I didn't put them on, I was sure to wear them when I was feeling particularly insecure or ugly. They didn't make me feel much more beautiful, but they were better at hiding the bald spots than anything else was.

When I was still living in the underclassmen dorm, my friends and I decided to throw a "roarin' twenties" party, complete with a trip to Chicago, which was a short train ride from our campus. The guys scoured Goodwill for zoot suits, fedoras, and thin shoes, while the women looked for dresses with sequins or flapper panels. I left the store with a blue knee-length dress adorned with three pounds of sequins and shoulder pads that had to be cut out.

As we were driving back from Goodwill, one of the girls came up with the idea of buying big false eyelashes for the night so we could all glam up. I felt sick.

We drove to the drugstore closest to campus, and I pretended to be clueless while the other girls tried to figure out where the falsies were. I already knew; in that particular drugstore chain, they were always in the back left corner of the store, next to the nail files and buffers.

My friends oohed and aahed over the false eyelashes, choosing the biggest, most dramatic ones they could find. I pretended to look at the lashes and took my time picking a big, feathery pair, but really I just wanted to leave. What if someone looked too closely at my eyelashes right then? Could they tell I was already wearing fake ones?

Thankfully, no one asked me anything. I tossed the pair on the checkout belt and sighed, repeating a payment I knew by heart: $5.49 plus tax. The girls around me were laughing at something and talking about what gum to try.

Back in the dorm, after we all got our dresses on, we squished in front of the bathroom mirror to put the glamorous false eyelashes on. I had taken off the pair of falsies I'd been wearing, knowing the girls would want to get ready together.

After jostling for a spot in front of the mirror with my friends, I took the new falsies out of their plastic case and, out of habit, began prepping the glue bottle in one hand with a lash in the other.

Melissa looked at me quizzically. "Ann, you look like you know what you're doing with those."

I glanced over at Jess. She smiled and raised her eyebrows at me, wondering how I would respond.

I shrugged, realizing that my autopilot motions had given me away. "I've worn them before."

Jess broke in. "What kind did you get, Mel? I got the reallllly long ones—they're so big!"

Melissa picked up her pair. "I got the ones with little jewels on the ends. *Sparkle!*"

That was it.

I glanced sideways at Jess and offered her a small grin, grateful she'd jumped in to derail Melissa's question. After a slow exhale, I pretended to fumble with the glue a little bit, and then I helped the other girls when they struggled with the delicate application.

I didn't want to tell them that I had been wearing falsies on and off for years, when things were worse rather than better. They wanted to wear the big feathery ones to look dramatic and sexy; I wasn't going to tell them that I wore the normal-grade ones regularly to hide what I'd done to myself. Instead, I talked about what shoes I should wear to match my dress.

We had a lot of fun in the city that night; our group of twenty went out to dinner downtown, talked in funny accents, got a lot of questions, and took some photos on the streets of Chicago. We probably looked like a theater cast out for a nighttime stroll. As we were talking and laughing and looking at the river that night, I realized that for the first time in a while, I wasn't worried about anyone noticing my eyelashes. All the other girls were wearing fake lashes; no one would stare longer at me than at anyone else because I was wearing them. It was a nice feeling; I felt normal.

Looking back, I now realize that *normal* is a construct; none of us are really normal, by any stretch. And in the grand scheme of things, I realize that thinking about my eyelashes so much might sound self-indulgent, ridiculous, petty. It's not that I wanted to focus on my eyelashes so much. It's just that I had come to define myself by what I lacked.

This idea of creating your identity around what you don't have may sound strange. But the woman who shuts her jaws against food because she lacks the number she wants on the scale will understand. The woman who looks longingly at the children on the playground when her own womb lacks a baby—she will understand. The single woman who feels pangs of envy and regret every time she sees another friend announce an engagement or a new relationship on social media will understand. It doesn't matter how big or small our lack seems to others—in our own hearts, that lack can loom large.

Living by What We Lack

Some scholars argue that perhaps the Bleeding Woman wasn't really an outcast. People were unclean all the time, they say—after a menstrual cycle or after sex or after touching a dead relative. They theorize that the Bleeding Woman's town, farther from the Temple, might not have been as particular in their observance of the law as communities closer to Jerusalem. Besides, it was a normal part of life to be occasionally unclean. So maybe she didn't face much in the way of social stigma; maybe she was just a bleeder who still got to spend time with her family and friends. Maybe, they say, it didn't really affect the outward trajectory of her life at all.

But even if her life hadn't been drastically impacted by her condition, the reality was that she was still bleeding—and she hated it. Why else would she have spent all she had to get better? She lost every penny to her name—hence her future—on doctors' bills. Even if others didn't mind that she was bleeding, she did. She wanted to be well.

No amount of historical study can give us a window into what it was like to live inside this woman's skin, what it felt like for her to define herself as a bleeder. Because once you see yourself as an outcast or as someone who doesn't fit in, the stigma doesn't need to come from anyone else. You carry it in your mind, in the folds of your persona. That's why you'll do anything to be normal again. It may not matter to anyone else that you lack what you desire. But it matters more than anything to you.

We all have lenses that we see ourselves through, whether good or bad. I saw myself through the lens of trich. Maybe you see yourself through the lens of some perceived failure—of not being smart enough, rich enough, good enough, happy enough, funny enough, or _____ enough.

When we start defining ourselves by what we lack, we obsess about it. We yearn for it, desire it above everything else. We play the mental game: *What would I give in return for a better job? What would I give in return for a size-four waist? What would I give in return for financial security? For a prettier face? For a husband? For a nice house? For a happy marriage? For a bigger platform? For an easier life? What would I give in return for* _____*?*

I once found myself incredulous that Esau would exchange his birthright for a mere bowl of stew (see Genesis 25:29-34). But I don't judge him so harshly anymore. When we experience that ravenous hunger for the one thing we so deeply desire, we all find ourselves tempted to give anything in exchange for it. We assume that getting that one thing we lack will be the key to permanently transforming our lives.

Telling Michael

Michael and I met and fell in love in college. We fell fast, hard, and wonderfully into love. I know it doesn't happen that way for everyone, but within three weeks, I knew he was the guy for me. And after several months, when we started talking and praying about marriage and a wedding and the future we wanted to build together, I knew something else.

I knew I needed to tell him.

I was scared. Michael had never given me a reason to distrust him, had never called me anything but beautiful. But I was afraid of letting him down. If I offered him my bare face, what would he see? Bald patches in my browline, a few eyelashes here and there. How could he possibly see me as beautiful?

First, I told him about trichotillomania. I explained the condition to him and told him that I'd had it for nearly a decade by the time we met. He listened, nodded at the appropriate times, and looked completely unfazed. "I'm so sorry, Ann. I'm sorry that it's so painful for you." He said all the right things. But I hadn't yet shown him my face without makeup.

Most of my girlfriends were around their boyfriends regularly without makeup on, but I believed that was a luxury they could afford since they all had long, full eyelashes. Their eyes didn't look stripped bare when they forgot—or chose to go without—mascara.

Then, a few weeks after I'd told Michael about trich, I decided it was time to let him see me without makeup. We were visiting my family for a long weekend in my childhood home, where so much of my journey with trich had started. After scrubbing off my makeup and staring at my face in the mirror for ten minutes, trying to see what Michael would see when I showed him my bald eyes, I walked into the living room, where he was studying. I felt I was offering him something defective.

He looked up from his study spot on the carpet, where he was lying on his stomach, sprawled out in three directions: an elegant *y*. He smiled at me and kept smiling as I came closer. I sat in front of him and crossed my legs. He looked up.

"This is me, without makeup."

He tilted his head and smiled, a little confused. "You look the same."

"No, I don't." I knew I didn't.

I took a deep breath and positioned myself for a push-up, leveling my eyes with his. The carpet was beige, with little ribbons of fabric in never-ending loops.

"These are my eyelashes. Without makeup." I closed my eyes, knowing that from above me, he would clearly see the empty spaces between my eyelashes. My ears were hot.

"Oh." His voice was quiet. "Yes. I can see." He ran his thumb across my left eyebrow. I opened my eyes.

"Ann, you're still beautiful." He looked at me, straight on. "I love you. It doesn't matter to me."

I felt my throat threatening to close. "Are you sure?" My words were a whisper.

"Ann, I love *you*. This doesn't define you." He held his hand to my cheek. "I will do whatever I can to help, but when it comes to our relationship, this doesn't change anything."

I put my head down, letting the loops imprint little lines on my cheek. I breathed. My tears drenched the carpet. "Thank you."

In Need of New Eyes

My parents, my sister, Jess, and Michael—the people who knew and loved me, who understood my condition—didn't look at me through the lens of trichotillomania. But I still saw myself as a puller. I saw that weakness, that brokenness, as the defining characteristic of who I was. I gauged my days based on how I fared with trich: Did I pull a lot? Or just a little? Did I fight against it? Or did I give in? Some of the biggest defeats in my entire life came during library study sessions in college, where I sat and pulled out eyelash after eyelash. I was so utterly defined by what I did to my body that I struggled to see myself as anything but broken.

But truly, I shouldn't have been so surprised by my lack of wholeness, by my inability to step out of that cycle on my own. As a Christian, I was acknowledging my need—my need for a Savior, my need for salvation. That's what I kept learning in my college theology and Bible courses over and over: that if there's one identifying mark of Christians, it's that we are a people who have admitted our inability to be whole on our own. In fact, we are a people who declare it every day: *I am not enough on my own. Only in Christ am I enough.*

But I struggled to experience that reality in my heart as well as in my mind. Experientially I understood how weak I was, and mentally I knew that I could even boast in my weaknesses. Still, I hated the *feeling* of being broken. It seemed so wrong. I don't think I'm alone in this—we all have a deep-down ache that we were made for more. We yearn to be whole. We always have, and on this side of heaven, I think we always will. The desire that C. S. Lewis writes about "to be united with the beauty we see, to pass into it, to receive it into ourselves"[6]—that's the desire so many of us have. It's not just a longing for external beauty, although we do long for that. It's a desire to be beautiful in the fullest sense. We long for our identity to be defined by beauty rather than weakness.

This is the tension of faith: Christ has promised us wholeness and redemption and resurrection, and in him, we have all the wholeness there is. But we don't live in it fully—yet. We feel our weaknesses acutely. Most of us hate those weaknesses. Some of us dwell on them. And when we start letting our weaknesses identify us—name us, mark us, brand us, slither into our worth and value—we fall prey to the lies of the enemy. When we listen to those lies, we allow our identity to be shaped by something other than Christ.

The apostle Paul—my friend in suffering and brokenness—writes to the church in Colossae about identity. He declares to them who they are—where their true identity is found:

> You, who were dead in your trespasses and the
> uncircumcision of your flesh, God made alive
> together with him, having forgiven us all our
> trespasses, by canceling the record of debt that

stood against us with its legal demands. This he set aside, nailing it to the cross. He disarmed the rulers and authorities and put them to open shame, by triumphing over them in him.

COLOSSIANS 2:13-15

Paul is reminding his readers—both the Colossian church and us—that our debts and trespasses, those ever-present sins and weaknesses, have been put on Jesus at the cross. We now have a new identity. We are no longer known by God as broken and sinful. Because Jesus took our shame, our sin, and our brokenness, our true identity is now found in him.

Paul continues this train of thought in the next chapter of Colossians:

If then you have been raised with Christ, seek the things that are above, where Christ is, seated at the right hand of God. Set your minds on things that are above, not on things that are on earth. For you have died, and your life is hidden with Christ in God.

COLOSSIANS 3:1-3

In Christ, we have become a new creation. Our old self has died (see Romans 6:6 and 2 Corinthians 5:17), and now our true life is hidden in Jesus. Our true life—our *truest* life, our very identity—is found in Christ. It makes sense to me why Paul paired these words about true identity with the charge to "set your minds on things that are above," because it's so easy to let the world, our flesh, and the enemy speak identity over us.

But here's the truth: Jesus has given us our true name, our true identity.

We are his beloved. We are *loved*.

He doesn't name me by my weakness, my sin, my brokenness. He doesn't name you by your weakness, your sin, your brokenness. Instead, he names us by what he has done for us. He names us by how he sees and knows us. He calls us his masterpiece (see Ephesians 2:10, NLT); he calls us his children (see John 1:12); he calls us his friends (see John 15:15); he calls us accepted (see Romans 15:7, NLT).

The truth is that when I was in college, trichotillomania didn't define me before God. No matter how much it felt like it did, trichotillomania didn't consume my identity. And the weaknesses and sins that I still struggle with today don't define me or consume my identity either.

God doesn't look at me and see what breaks me. He looks at me and sees a child who has been loved, accepted, and redeemed.

I wish I could go back and hug that Ann in college and stand by her when she looked in the mirror and saw her lash line, thin and empty and damaged by her own hands, the Ann who defined herself as a puller. To the Ann who defined herself by what she lacked—lacking eyelashes, lacking self-control, lacking the ability to be healed—I would tell her this: *God looks at you through eyes of compassion and sees what he has already given to you: a new name, a new identity.*

I would tell that college-aged version of me to keep asking God for healing but to go even further than that: *Ask him to give you spiritual eyes—eyes that allow you to see and identify yourself not by your brokenness but rather by his love and power.*

If I were to meet a version of my college self, I would pray Paul's prayer for the Ephesian church over her:

For this reason, because I have heard of your
faith in the Lord Jesus and your love toward all
the saints, I do not cease to give thanks for you,
remembering you in my prayers, that the God of
our Lord Jesus Christ, the Father of glory, may give
you the Spirit of wisdom and of revelation in the
knowledge of him, *having the eyes of your hearts
enlightened*, that you may know what is the hope to
which he has called you, what are the riches of his
glorious inheritance in the saints, and what is the
immeasurable greatness of his power toward us who
believe, according to the working of his great might
that he worked in Christ when he raised him from
the dead and seated him at his right hand in the
heavenly places, far above all rule and authority and
power and dominion, and above every name that is
named, not only in this age but also in the one to
come. And he put all things under his feet and gave
him as head over all things to the church, which is
his body, the fullness of him who fills all in all.

EPHESIANS 1:15-23 (EMPHASIS ADDED)

Paul prayed for enlightenment in "the eyes of [our] hearts," and that makes a lot of sense to me. When I was in college, my eyes and my heart were the two parts of me that tended to get tangled up. I needed a transformation in the way I perceived myself. And while that transformation didn't happen overnight, as I look back, I can see that God was in the process of changing the eyes of my heart so I could define myself not by what I lacked but by who loved me: Jesus himself.

He was starting to give me new eyes. In every way.

CHAPTER 5

When Waiting
Feels Offensive

*H*ope rose occasionally—barely, remotely—in the places of Sarah's soul that had not yet been completely darkened by sorrow. It had bubbled when a doctor or midwife recommended a new technique to try to stop the blood; it had swelled when unbidden dreams of a future with a husband and a family flashed before her eyes. But these days, hope fluttered less often. Twelve years had passed since the bleeding started, and now, at twenty-six, Sarah knew she had little reason left to hope. She strained to pinpoint the cause of her suffering. Had she done something wrong in her childhood? But if she had offended God to bring about such anguish, she had never intended to. Whatever the cause, this fact remained: almost all that she had ever hoped for had been taken away.

Still, there was one grace Sarah was thankful for: Lydia.

Like many others, Lydia had been Sarah's friend before the bleeding started. Unlike everyone else, Lydia remained Sarah's friend even when the bleeding became a public affair. She declared that she did not care what anyone else thought and that Sarah should not either. Even when Lydia wed and started bearing babies, she brought her children over to play with Sarah and encouraged her to hold them and sing to them. Sarah did not know if Lydia told her husband that she went to an unclean woman's home; she never asked.

One bright Tuesday afternoon, Lydia came by unannounced, as she always did. Lydia was tired, Sarah could tell. Three babies in twice as many years had left her with little sleep. And so as soon as she ducked under the frame of the home, Lydia held out Malachi, her three-month-old son, for Sarah to hold.

Sarah shook her head. "I do not want to give him my curse."

Lydia's eyes narrowed, the dark brown of her irises glowing like embers from the fire. "You are ridiculous, Sarah. You will give no curse to my children because you carry no curse."

"What, then, do I carry?" The defeat in Sarah's voice was unmistakable.

Lydia softened. "You carry a burden. That is all." She pushed Malachi into Sarah's chest.

Sarah lodged the baby on her hip and started to sway, moving in order to keep herself from speaking. There was a lump in her throat, and if she spoke, she knew she would start crying. Enough tears had been shed these past twelve years, and she did not want to cry anymore. She was tired of crying. She was tired of hoping. She was tired, she suddenly realized, of living.

Lydia spoke softly. "Sarah, there is a holy man nearby, a man who performs miracles. Have you heard of him?"

Sarah shook her head. She stroked Malachi's cheek, taking in his softness. She had once had dreams for a family of her own. A tear rolled down her cheek; she could not help it.

Lydia's voice grew in intensity. "He is a healer, Sarah. I have heard stories—stories nearly past believing. He has freed men from demons. He has cleansed—even touched*—lepers."*

Sarah put her hand on Malachi's head. She felt the hair on her arms bristle. What kind of holy man would touch a leper?

"It has been said that this rabbi has even raised a boy from the dead. From the dead!*"*

Sarah handed Malachi back to Lydia. She felt light headed; she had never heard of anyone like this. Could it even be true?

"Who is this man?" She was surprised at the optimism in her own voice.

"His name is Jesus," Lydia said. "Jesus of Nazareth." Her eyes shone. "He might be coming to our town."

Unbidden, Sarah felt her heart beat faster. The feeling was odd, uncomfortable. She hardly knew that feeling anymore. It was a surge of hope.

During the last two years of college, I started to get a little restless spiritually. For the first time, I'd been reading the Bible all the way through, and the more I read, the less satisfied I became about my condition. I read about Jesus giving his Spirit to his disciples. I read about Jesus healing sick people and raising people from the dead and multiplying food. And then I read Jesus' words that those who believe in him would do "greater works than these" (John 14:12). I was confused. Was Jesus being literal or figurative?

In my English classes, my professors talked openly about the different genres found in the biblical text, but I was sure Jesus' words were never considered fiction (at least, not within orthodox theology). And contextually, when Jesus spoke these words to his followers, he wasn't speaking in parables. If I took him at his word, how could I not look for more than I was currently experiencing? For healing? For wholeness? I wanted to experience more. I wanted to know God more.

It was in reading the books of Elisabeth Elliot that I tasted some of that *more*. She is perhaps best known as a missionary and the wife of the martyred missionary Jim Elliot, and while her life overseas deeply inspired me, it was her books about living as a Christian that impacted me the most. As I immersed myself in her writings, she quickly became one of my heroes, and during my junior year, I lived in the same dormitory on campus that she'd lived in as a student nearly sixty years earlier.

One day I climbed the steps two at a time from my first-floor dorm room to the fourth floor of the old building, the top level of what students called "the nunnery" or "the red castle." At the time, the building was a female-only dorm, and it looked like a red mansion—thus the monikers. I arrived out of breath, but when I looked through the glass, I was glad I'd made the trip.

The room was empty.

I tucked my book, journal, and Bible under my arm and pushed on the door handle. This room at the top of the building was the dormitory "chapel." It was the size of two or three normal rooms and held a few couches covered in old floral patterns, probably throwbacks from several generations ago. A deep-hued wooden case filled with books stood on one side of the room, and the tall windows, covered by sheer white curtains, overlooked the snowy heart of campus below.

I loved being here; I was fairly certain that Elisabeth Elliot had spent time in this chapel too. I wanted to know God in the same place—and hopefully in some of the same ways—that she had.

As the snow swirled and laced through the sky that winter of my junior year, I found myself hungry to know more of God. I would sit on those floral couches in my gray sweatpants and read, stretching out my legs on the cushions and soaking in the words of Scripture and the words of Elisabeth Elliot back to back. Other times I got on my knees in that room, my forearms pressed into the couch, my feet tucked underneath me. I asked God to meet me there, to encounter me with his love, to let me know more of him. I prayed for healing. I prayed for his touch.

I read Elliot's book *Passion and Purity* ravenously, gulping it down in great portions, trying to slake my thirst for more of God and how to live for him. Her words stung me in the best way, barbs of truth that cut to my heart and taught me my own thoughts:

I realized that the deepest spiritual lessons are not learned by His letting us have our way in the end, but by His making us wait, bearing with us in love and patience until we are able honestly to pray what He taught His disciples to pray: Thy will be done.[1]

Waiting. Spiritual lessons. Yes. It was always trich that I was waiting for healing from, but what spiritual lessons was God teaching me in the midst of it? I couldn't tell. I searched for other bits of wisdom from Elliot's writings and came across this quote that stirred and scared me:

God never withholds from His child that which His love and wisdom call *good*. . . . God's refusals are always merciful—"severe mercies" at times, as St. Augustine recognized (Confessions XI, 25), but mercies all the same.[2]

I didn't know what to do with these words emotionally, although mentally I could assent to their truth. When it came to trichotillomania, I knew that God *could* heal me, and yet I knew that up until now—in the decade I'd had with trich—he had not. Was his refusal of my healing a mercy? *Really?* It felt more like a curse.

I couldn't square it away in my heart. Because what could be better than healing? The more I encountered Jesus on the pages of Scripture, the more I saw that he was *always* healing, always making people new. So why wouldn't he heal me? Certainly this would be a small thing for him to do, this God-man who had given sight to the blind and raised people from the dead. What would it cost him to heal me?

Nothing, I reasoned. It would cost him nothing.

So why wouldn't he?

I couldn't make sense of it, and because I couldn't understand his reasons for withholding healing, I vacillated between hope and something else.

I teetered on the edge of offense.

Stripped Bare

Churches often advertised their conferences on our small campus. Most of the time I ignored the posters, knowing I wouldn't have the time or energy to head off campus for the evening when I could be studying or sleeping (or, let's be honest, goofing off with friends). But a well-known speaker was coming in to town for a conference at a local church, and Michael and I, along with several friends, decided to go to the Thursday evening session.

We were excited to hear this woman speak about the work of God in a different corner of the world where she was a missionary, and I went with an expectant heart. I knew there would be time for prayer at the end of the session, and brick by brick, the desire had been building in me to ask for healing—to ask someone else to pray for me to be healed. My family had been praying for years, I had been praying, Jess had been praying, and now Michael was praying. But my heart jumped at the hope that perhaps this speaker might be able to pray for me—and that through her prayer, I might be set free. Why did I put such stock in her? For no other reason than I was desperate to be made well and here was a new chance to ask for healing.

I honestly don't remember much about what the speaker said about her mission halfway across the world; I don't remember much about the praying and singing. My heart pattered in my chest much of the night. I believed that Jesus could heal me and hoped that maybe, if I stepped out in faith, *tonight could be the night.* I didn't tell Michael or any of my friends that I wanted to ask the speaker to pray for me to be rid of trichotillomania. I didn't even know if she would be praying for people or—if she did—if I could get to her in such a large room.

Still, I wanted to try.

When the singing was over, the speaker invited anyone who desired prayer to come forward—for salvation, for hope, for healing. I nearly ran forward, threading through people and chairs to get to the front.

And I got my turn. Over the hum of others singing to Jesus, the speaker asked me what I wanted prayer for. The words tumbled out in a mix of fear and expectation.

"I have this condition—trichotillomania—where I pull out my own eyelashes. I can't stop. I've had it for a decade, and I want to be free."

She angled her chin away from me. "Did you have an abusive parent?"

What? I snapped my head up in alarm. That was the last thing I'd expected her to say. "No! No, not at all."

I stood there, my face a knot in front of her.

And then this woman started praying to cast a demon out of me.

"We cast out this evil spirit in the name of Jesus!"

I froze.

"Be gone from her and stop tormenting her, in Jesus' name! Jesus, cleanse this woman!" She continued to yell over me, casting out some demon she assumed I harbored in my bones.

My ears burned fire-hot, and I tasted the salty tears that were running down my cheeks—not because I'd been touched by the Spirit, but because I was so horrified. I knew that I struggled with trich and with weakness and with sin—but to have someone assume I was demon possessed because of my condition?

I was undone.

All my unspoken fears about what people might think when I told them that I had trich were confirmed in that instant.

Her prayer was a curse rather than a blessing.

She moved on to pray with someone else, and although no one else heard her words over me, I felt stripped bare in front of the crowd. Angry and trembling, I dashed away, unsure of what had just happened to me. I had no words then to explain it to Michael, let alone to anyone else. My heart clamored for something solid to cling to, but I didn't know what to think—about myself, about my condition, about this woman. Did I actually have a demon prowling around inside me? Was I so far past healing that I needed an exorcism?

I felt clawed. Raw.

I wept through the rest of the night. Was this my reward for hope? Was this my reward for faith?

Hope Deferred

Even before asking for prayer that night, I knew the truth: God doesn't always grant healing. And yet as I read through the Bible and as my hunger for God grew, I had come to a place where I was more full of faith that he *could* heal me than ever before. The Jesus I prayed to was the same Jesus who had walked the streets of ancient cities, healing everyone who came to him, leaving no one sick or infirm or mute. Like the Bleeding Woman, I had the faith that if I could get close enough to him—if my fingers could just graze his robe— I could finally get what I had been praying for.

But I still knew, deep down, that God doesn't always grant healing or help in the ways we want him to. He doesn't always respond the way we wish he would; it's a truth I still see unfolding before me most days of the week. My friend Allison has lost more babies than have been born to her— she has walked through half a dozen miscarriages. And dear friends of ours have been church planting for years, yet every month they struggle financially. I have friends who deal with Crohn's disease, with ulcers that won't disappear, with mental anguish too deep to name. I have seen marriages split up, fall apart, dissipate under the weight of pain and sorrow and hurt. These are all people of faith, people who know and love and follow Jesus.

As for me, for all the faith I had in his ability to heal, God

ANN SWINDELL

didn't heal me that night—or during the rest of my years in college. He didn't keep Allison's babies growing in her womb. He hasn't blessed our friends with abundant finances. He doesn't always bring marriages back from the brink or guarantee deliverance for troubled minds. I don't know why. God's ways, it says in Scripture, are above our ways. His thoughts are not our thoughts (see Isaiah 55:8). It's hard to wrestle with a God who doesn't bend to our desires, even our seemingly good desires. And it's not that God doesn't hear. He is not deaf, nor is he powerless (see Isaiah 59:1). He is, in fact, compassionate. Unendingly compassionate. He overflows with unshakable, unbending love. My favorite psalm in all of Scripture—perhaps my favorite chapter in all of the Bible—declares this about God's character:

The Lord is merciful and gracious,
slow to anger and abounding in steadfast love.
PSALM 103:8

God is good. *Good.* He is not a trickster, and he is not mean (see Matthew 7:7-11). He holds the world together, and he is for us, not against us (see Romans 8:31).

But sometimes it's hard to reconcile that truth with reality. Sometimes it's hard to look at the brokenness and pain and struggle in the world and still trust that God is good. In my college years, I often wrestled with the truth of what I knew cognitively: that God could heal me instantaneously—a small thing for him, surely—and the truth that he didn't. So my daily struggle with the shame of trich continued.

And there were times when offense crept into my heart and leapfrogged my hope, my tenderness, even my faith.

One day when I felt my offense toward God mounting, I headed to "Gold Star": the prayer chapel in the student center. The air was still in the prayer chapel; I loved this place but hated the feelings I had that day. I was sitting in one of the pews, pouring angry, hasty words onto the pages of my journal with dark strokes of ink. I told God that he seemed mean and cold and distant and impossible to deal with. I trembled there with eyelashes scattered across the pages, angry and ashamed that the lashes were no longer where they should have been.

I looked up to study the stained glass windows in the chapel. There was no sunlight in this interior room of the student center; instead, the windows were illuminated by electric lights that glowed behind them. One of the pieces was a free-form style of stained glass, with huge shards of color that overlapped and melted together to create an image of the Prodigal Son returning home. The father faced me, embracing his child. The scene was scattered with reds, purples, and yellows. I had to look at the image closely to really see it—the joyful hug from the father, the sagging relief of the son. The other stained glass, on the left, was a traditional scene, clearly outlined in lead and illuminated with greens, whites, and blues. It was Jesus, holding a lamb in his arms. Jesus, the Good Shepherd, the one who carries.

"I don't feel carried, Jesus. I don't feel taken care of. I hardly feel seen."

No one else was in the chapel. The silence hung like a cloak around me.

The tears I cried over trich weren't new to me, but there in the chapel, they felt surprisingly fresh. "I keep asking this question, God. Why? Why won't you heal me? My hours of praying and begging, even my days of fasting—what have they done? Anything?"

I answered the question myself: "Nothing! They've done nothing! I'm still here with eyelashes on my journal, and I'm worse than I've ever been!"

I shifted my gaze back to the father and the Prodigal Son. I couldn't see the son's face, buried as it was in the father's chest. The lines of the father's face were intentionally muted, purposely vague. "When it comes to trich, has it made any difference that I'm your child? Does it matter that I'm yours if you won't answer this one prayer I keep begging you to answer, this problem I keep begging you to fix?"

The tears ran down my face, wetting the pages of my journal, blurring my vision. I was crying now, but not with God. I was crying *at* him, against him. I wanted to push him away—this God who is all places and everywhere—and I wanted to run from him.

That was how I started to understand how people become bitter, how the seeds of anger turn into deep roots of dismissal when it comes to trusting God. Petty as my own little world might have been, it was the only world I had. If God wouldn't show up there, in the middle of my life, how else could I know him?

Those were ugly days, battered days, when I protested

to God and yelled at him. I'm not proud of my anger or the ways I fought him. My words in those journals some days were bitter, willful, too much to carry. But it is the truth: I was mad. More than that.

I was offended.

Offense or Obedience

I can only imagine how the Bleeding Woman perceived God after twelve years of being unable to participate in any religious ceremonies. She was considered unclean, which meant she couldn't be in holy places. One scholar notes that until women went through "purification" of their uncleanness from bleeding, they were "banished from the community."[3] This woman would have been perpetually banished, which makes me think her opportunity for offense would have been great. For not only was she unclean, unable to participate in the regular rhythms of community life, but anyone who touched her also would be made unclean.

According to the law, anyone who "came into contact with [a woman] during menstruation would be banished until evening." Historical writings indicate that the ruling of the Temple being closed to bleeding women "was carefully observed in Jesus' day."[4] The law was still alive and well—and that meant that the Bleeding Woman was on the outskirts of life as an Israelite.

And it wasn't like she had a second option. The only way her people had to know Yahweh was to be part of the communal life of God through Temple and ceremony and synagogue and festival. How then must the Bleeding Woman have understood God? As a God she wasn't allowed to worship? As a God whose rules kept her from her community? Perhaps she saw him as harsh and difficult and uncaring. Perhaps she assumed he was distant and hard hearted. Perhaps she thought he didn't love her. The Bleeding Woman could have easily chosen offense and anger. The Bible doesn't tell us if she chose offense with God, so we can only conjecture. But at some point, she would have had to deliberately choose to walk away from him or to continue to trust him.

When we have begged and demanded from God all that we can, and when he still doesn't change our situation, we're left with a choice: we can choose offense with him, or we can choose obedience.

Offense is a terror of a thing: it puts us in the judgment seat over God. It sets us in the place of declaring what he should do and how he should work. And then, when he doesn't do what we think he should—when he won't bow to our ways of understanding—the stance of offense tricks us into thinking we have a right to condemn God. We strong-arm God, we yell at him, we tell him all the things he's not. We point our finger at him and tell him he's wrong. We tell him how the world *really* is; we sneer that he isn't being God the way that he should be.

And while it's good to be honest with God, there is a distinct difference between heartfelt honesty and hostile honesty. Heartfelt honesty comes to God on its knees. Hostile honesty comes to God pointing a finger. And if we let our honesty turn hostile—if we become offended enough—we will walk away. We will judge God and choose to go on without him.

It would have been mighty easy for the Bleeding Woman to choose offense with God based on her circumstances alone. She could have protested against him and bludgeoned his name in her heart with her words and her anger. And perhaps she did.

But I don't think so. I don't think she chose offense.

I think she kept her heart open to God. I think she kept obeying his commands. She must have had doubts and questions, but I think she allowed the flame of hope to burn in her—however small it was—that he was good and that he heard her prayers. She believed with her whole heart that this traveling rabbi Jesus could heal her, and I think it took great hope and tenderness for her to have that kind of faith. To believe that anyone could still heal her after all the doctors had mangled her case and after all the money she'd spent with no healing to show for it—what a softhearted response! What room she had made for faith and hope when everything in her life pressed for bitterness and rage!

She kept her heart open to the possibility that she could be healed and that this Jesus could be her healer. In spite of her unwanted sickness, and in spite of her futile attempts to change her situation, the Bleeding Woman lived her life without turning away from God. She made her choice, and she chose obedience rather than offense.

The Lingering Whys

I had a choice too: Would I choose offense with God for not healing me yet again? For not answering my prayer? For letting the missionary speaker spiritually attack me when what

I needed was a word of comfort, a prayer of hope? From my own perspective, I couldn't see any reason why God wouldn't heal me, why he wouldn't change my struggle into a victorious cure. Wouldn't he get all the glory? All the doctors and therapies and supplements hadn't helped me, so clearly he would get the attention and fame if he healed me. Wouldn't he show himself to be God when no one else could heal?

Why wouldn't he heal me? *Why?*

I don't know.

I had no answer for the *whys* in my heart and in my head. God seemed to be silent when it came to that question.

What I do know is that in his mercy, God pulled me back from the crag of offense to his truth and his kindness. This was a gift to me, although I couldn't see it for what it was at the time.

This wooing of my heart and softening of my spirit happened in two ways.

The first way was through a woman named Nita, the wife of one of my professors. Nita had started mentoring me the summer after my freshman year in college, and hers is a friendship I still treasure today. During those college years, she and I met twice a month to talk about my walk with Jesus, to discuss the Word, and to pray.

We were in her home one afternoon, sitting at the small table in the kitchen, warming our hands around full cups of Earl Grey. Nita was the one who taught me to drink tea—and enjoy it—and every time I went to her house, she served me from one of the dainty tea sets that lived in her glass hutch.

Tiny lilies hugged the rim of the teacup, which looked like it had been dipped in a light blue the color of winter mornings.

When we talked that afternoon, my heart came tumbling out. There was a phone attached to the kitchen wall, and when I couldn't hold Nita's gaze anymore, I remember looking at the white coil dripping down that wall in a grand loop. I struggled to look her in the face because what I was sharing burned so deeply and so painfully.

I didn't tell Nita about trichotillomania directly. I was beating around the bush, talking about all the disappointment I held against God. The frustration and the hurt were piled like a tower of building blocks on my insides. Each time God hadn't answered my prayers the way I asked, my heart had added another block to the wobbly turret. That day, the more I talked to Nita, the more the frustration built, and my heart couldn't withstand the pressure. The blocks came tumbling down, and I started crying at the kitchen table, all my insides and my outsides meshing in tears and confusion. I was a mess. And yet what I remember most is not what Nita said but what she did.

She put her hand over mine at that kitchen table, and she cried with me.

Nita sat with me in that place of disappointment and hurt. She didn't chastise me or immediately correct me. Instead, she communed with me. Her hand and her silence let me know that I was allowed to feel those emotions in my relationship with God. She didn't force me to be anywhere other than where I was.

We sat together at the kitchen table and cried for a while, her hand on mine. I didn't try to move it away. Nita always carried tissues in her purse, and she dug out two and handed one to me.

She tapped the corners of her eyes with the tissue and waited until my tears subsided. When she spoke, her voice was a violin: wavering with emotion but full of deep conviction. "We don't always understand what God does or doesn't do. But we always know—we *always know*—that he loves us." She squeezed my hand. I squeezed it back.

I let out a shaky breath of air. My voice was quiet. "It just makes the *no* harder to hear sometimes, because I don't understand why that's his answer. It's hard for me to reconcile his love with the *no*."

"I understand, Ann. I do." I recalled the stories from her own life that she had shared with me—the losses she had endured, the sorrows she had walked through—and I knew that she *did* understand. Her eyes were glossy, and she took a big breath before speaking again. "Who shall separate us from the love of Christ?" (Romans 8:35).

I knew the passage in Romans she was referring to, and I shook my head. "Nothing, Nita." My voice was a whisper. "Nothing and no one." *Not even a no.*

Nita's kindness and truth spoke blessing to me in the place where the speaker's exorcism had been a curse. It began to heal up some of that wound.

And this is what healed up much of the rest: reading the Word and spending time in God's presence. This was the second way the Lord softened my heart. As I kept returning to God and seeking him, he met with me.

There was no magic formula that took me from the brink of offense to tenderness with Jesus again. It simply entailed daily time with him, reading the Bible, praying, and journaling my heart to him between the lines in my notebook. This was the practice I had started, and it became my lifeline. I found that as I kept spending time with Christ, I couldn't harden my heart against him. It hurt sometimes, reading those stories in Scripture about others who were healed and knowing it wasn't yet my own story. But Jesus met me in that place, over and over, and I came to terms with my own need for him. I embraced the gift of being his—even if he wasn't answering me the way I wanted.

One Saturday afternoon in the prayer chapel, I had the space to myself, and I sat in the silence, thinking and talking with God in my head. After a while, I stretched out on one of the pews and stared at the ceiling while I asked him more questions in my heart, not really expecting any answers. Me and God—I was alone and yet together with him.

I closed my eyes, and when I did, an image entered my mind—one that was clear and sharp. Jesus and I were climbing the side of a red mountain together. With shafts of rock jutting out, the mountain offered only small handholds and footholds. My struggle was clear: in trying to climb the mountain, I had reached the point of exhaustion and was unsure if I could keep going. Jesus was just ahead of me—above me—and we were near the top. He extended his arm and pulled me the rest of the way up the mountain, until we made it to a clearing.

When we made it to the flat top of the mountain, I saw that we were at the cross. Jesus was hanging on it, but Jesus was also right next to me. Two Jesuses.

The Jesus who had helped me climb the mountain— really, who had climbed the last bit for both of us—sat down beside me just a few yards from the cross. We sat with our knees tucked up to our chins, so close to each other that not even wind passed between our shoulders. Then Jesus pointed to the cross with him still hanging on it. The Jesus on the cross was mangled, bloody, and caved in around his own chest.

The Jesus next to me spoke. "I did this for you, Ann." He was looking at me, smiling so broadly that I smiled back, even with such pain in front of both of us. "I am *so glad* I could do it for you."

And then it was over. I opened my eyes, and I knew in the center of my soul that Jesus loved me—really. I knew that I was on his heart when he died on the cross and that—more incredibly—he wasn't mad about the fact that he had to die for me.

My offense washed away in light of his love.

That is what love does: it casts out fear. My offense, borne from the fear that I might never be healed, made me feel that I was strange and unwhole because of my struggle with trich. But when I awoke to his love, that fear was stilled. It was silenced. It was gone.

Every hour I spent in the prayer chapel, every morning I

woke up to read the Word—it was in those small, daily acts that I encountered God's heart on the pages of Scripture and that I met afresh with the one who had given his very life for me. I came to know his life and his love not solely as words on a page but as hope spoken directly to my heart. And I found, maybe fully for the first time, that all I really had was Jesus, and to walk away from him in offense would be more devastating than continuing to deal with trich.

If I couldn't have healing, I knew I could still have Christ. He would be enough for me.

The Choice We All Must Make

What God was asking of me in college—and what he asks of all of us, every day of our lives—is obedience in place of offense. Obedience enables us to keep putting one foot of faith in front of the other, even when we feel no affection for God. It's the act of doing what we know to be true even when there's no emotion behind it. It's saying yes to him even when we don't understand what he is doing—or what he isn't doing. Ultimately, it's trusting God through action and confession even when our hearts feel dead.

It's a hard truth: to have a Savior who doesn't always explain what he does or make it easy to follow him. It's hard to follow a King who won't always decree what we want. It's hard to obey a Lord whose ways are higher than mine, a Lord who doesn't think like I do (see Isaiah 55:8-9). Put simply, I often don't understand him.

But I decided to accept Jesus' hard teaching—that he is "the way, and the truth, and the life" (John 14:6)—even when he wouldn't do what I wanted him to do and when he wouldn't be coerced by my tears and my anger. Yes, I got hurt and frustrated and angry about what he wouldn't do for me. And yet I always came back to this: God is God, and he loves me and cares for me. Why he wouldn't heal me, I didn't pretend to know. But where else could I go (see John 6:68)? He *is* the Word of Life.

CHAPTER 6

When Waiting
Brings You Shame

On her sleeping mat, Sarah turned onto her side and curled into a tight ball. In the darkness, her thoughts turned to everything she wanted to forget. So much had happened in the twelve years since she started bleeding. The opportunities for marriage had come and gone, waved away by her father. At first, he said that he was not ready to part with his child, that her suitors should come back in another year. Then in two. Eventually the potential beaus—and their families—stopped coming. By the time Sarah was eighteen, there was a quiet assumption around town that something was wrong with her.

Something was wrong; she had realized it when the worry settled into her mother's eyes the way chalkiness settled into the eyes of very old men. She could never marry in this state because she could

115

never consummate a marriage, and no man wanted a wife who could bear no children and give no pleasure.

Sarah looked up into the darkness. She could not sleep. Something about what Lydia had said about the holy man—about Jesus of Nazareth—stirred her. The night was stagnant, but her heart was churning, and she knew the emotion for what it was: hope. That fluttering feeling had nearly died in her, and she tried to push against the feeling, tried to force it away. Surely the rumors about this rabbi were simply the bloated stories of gossiping women. The people always clamored for a new prophet, a new messiah. They had all been wrong before.

But the way Lydia talked about him—the stories she recounted—made Jesus of Nazareth sound different. Touching lepers? No one did that, not if they valued their lives and their reputations. Especially not rabbis.

Sarah uncoiled her body and turned on her back. Maybe he really was a healer. A shock of hope sped down her spine. If only I could touch his robe.

Sarah shook her head. Even the thought of touching him made her ashamed, and she felt her cheeks tingle in the navy warmth of the night. She could never approach a holy man, let alone touch him. She would make him unclean.

But what if he did not know she had touched him? What if no one knew? The hope inside her was ricocheting now, overflowing, and for the first time in years, Sarah did not push it away. Without trying to, she began to form a plan.

I will slip into the crowd behind him. I will keep my head and my face covered; no one will expect to see me anyway. It has been so many years, perhaps the town has forgotten me. *Her heart surged with hope and pain.* Yes, I will come up behind him, and I will touch the hem of his robe. That is where their power resides, I know. Every story I heard in the marketplace as a child spoke of the power in the hems of the rabbis. I will not shame my family or the rabbi. I will simply be invisible, and once I touch his robe, I will run away.

And then Sarah realized: either way, she must do this. She would risk open shame for the chance at healing.

For if she was healed, all her suffering would be over. And if she was caught and shamed and died of a broken heart, all her suffering would be over then, too.

Sarah made her decision. She would find the rabbi, and she would touch the hem of his robe. That is what she would do.

That is what she must do.

Shame is the creature I carried on my back for years.

In a culture that values strength, the realities of weakness, brokenness, and struggle can infuse a quiet poison into the heart—the poison of shame. And shame was something I'd felt since that first day with trich when I was eleven years old. I felt like a failure, unable to stop doing the one thing I hated. And I was ashamed that I was apparently too weak to overcome my condition.

Shame is a common thread when it comes to trichotillo-mania. One specialist writes:

[Trichotillomania] is associated with feelings of depression, shame, anxiety and disgust. . . .

For the trichotillomania population, the shame experienced with this act is generally associated with the belief that others will notice the perceivable hair loss produced by [pulling]. . . . A great deal of time and effort is generally dedicated toward concealing or masking the effects of the hair loss.[1]

I know these feelings, these choices. I dedicated time, money, and effort to concealing the effects of trich. But no matter what I did, it resulted in the same outcome every time: shame.

Feeling like a Failure

Michael and I married a couple of weeks after my college graduation. By God's grace, I was in an easier season with trich, and I felt comfortable enough to wear just mascara on our wedding day. It felt like a victory for me, one that only a handful of people really understood.

Six months after our wedding, one of my best friends from college was having her own wedding in Florida. I was a bridesmaid, and money was tight for us as newlyweds. Michael was still finishing his undergraduate degree, and I had started graduate school, so we couldn't afford for both of us to go to the celebration. I would be going by myself and sharing a hotel room with Jess (a fellow bridesmaid in the wedding) and a few other college acquaintances.

Trich had gotten increasingly worse for me in those

early months of marriage; perhaps the stress of my first job out of college combined with the start of graduate school, navigating life as a newlywed, and the reality of bills was too much for my body and brain to handle. At any rate, I was pulling a lot, and I looked worse than I had in a long time. Anxiety, worry, and stress all compounded into my plucking out lots and lots of lashes and brows. Michael was unendingly kind to me, and I know that he truly saw me as beautiful, but I recoiled over the thought of seeing so many of my good friends at the wedding when my eyelashes looked so horrible. I felt deeply ashamed of what I'd done to myself.

This was right around the time when the salons in our area started advertising long-lasting lash extensions as a way to glam up for a big event or weekend. They were semi-permanent, glued-on fake lashes that licensed aestheticians applied to each individual lash, therefore extending the appearance of eyelashes and making them look longer and fuller.

I felt a little hope—hope that these lashes might make me look beautiful and might keep me from pulling any more out. I reasoned that if I spent money on getting the semi-permanent falsies, maybe I could get over the hump of this bad season with trichotillomania.

But the cost, in that time of life, felt exorbitant. The price was around $150 for a full set of lashes, and for us, that amount would pay for more than a week's worth of groceries and gas. Michael had to work fifteen hours at the coffee shop to make that much; it was a luxury we couldn't really afford.

We would have to dip into our savings for this, and even then, I didn't know if the new falsies would work.

But the desire for *something* to work—the hope that this might be a real help—won out, and I talked with Michael about it. He hugged me and, knowing the cost, told me to go for it. I scheduled the appointment, and a few days before I flew to Florida for the wedding, I headed to the salon to get the extensions.

I was nervous that the aesthetician might ask why my eyelashes were so sparse, but she seemed unfazed. I mentioned something about not having a lot of lashes, and she replied that one of her clients had nearly ripped all of hers out using a bad curling wand. I wondered if, actually, that other client had trich too. *All of us make up stories,* I thought.

After an hour on my back, I walked out of the salon $150 poorer but with a fuller and darker lash line. I felt encouraged—even hopeful. *Maybe,* I thought as I drove home, *this will be the fix I need to stop pulling and to get my lashes back to normal!*

I admired my new lashes in the mirror; they definitely weren't thick, as I didn't have many lashes for the aesthetician to adhere the fake ones to. However, they were longer, and overall, my lashes looked more normal than they had in months. I felt hesitantly optimistic about this whole experiment.

The hope itself felt new. The longer I'd dealt with trichotillomania, the harder it had become for me to believe that it would ever end. It wasn't for lack of wanting to believe—it's just that hope was harder and harder to come by. I knew I was going to need a miracle. I knew that no doctor, no medicine, no therapy was going to "fix" me. The only way for me to get better was to receive a touch from Jesus himself. But I hoped that these lashes would at least help me, even if they couldn't heal me. Maybe they would keep me from getting worse.

So I went to Florida and cried on the plane, already missing my new husband. But when I landed, I landed to Elsie, the beaming bride-to-be, and Jess, whom I'd missed so much in those six months. Our first day in sunny Miami was wonderful. We hung out by the pool in the backyard of Elsie's family home, and I drank up the sunshine like water, adoring the warmth on my skin after the start of winter in Chicago. The wedding rehearsal glowed with love and joy, and they served more food at the rehearsal dinner than I could eat—steak and lobster and bread and cake. We toasted and celebrated; I laughed so hard at dinner that I cried through all my mascara, which I was wearing on top of my lashes.

It was a wonderful start to the weekend.

But that night, after the celebration, I found myself lying awake in the hotel bedroom, toying with the new lashes. They felt different from the falsies I was used to—harder, pointier, thicker. Soon I found myself pulling. I pulled out five, then ten, then twenty, then thirty of those expensive eyelashes—and with them, my own lashes, glued as a base to their fibers. As I lay there in the dark, thoughts ran through my head over and over and over:

I wasted our money. So much money, all for nothing!

I'm such a failure. Again! I'm always a failure!

I'm going to look so ugly in the morning, with the falsies gone and my bare lashes worse than before! This is exactly what I was afraid of, and now it has happened.

These lashes aren't helping like I thought they would—they're making me worse.

I'm so ashamed of how I look, of what I've done to myself. I'll never be free.

It was nearly midnight. The thoughts were overwhelming me, overtaking me. I rolled out of bed and grabbed my cell phone and my room key. I started dialing Michael before I even made it out the door.

I slunk down against the wall outside our room and pulled my knees up to my chest. The carpet was a mix of browns and muted oranges, diamonds upon diamonds leading all the way to the elevator. I was in tears before Michael picked up.

"Honey? Are you okay?" I'd woken him up, and I heard the fear in his voice.

"I'm okay, but I just pulled out all my fake eyelashes that we paid so much money for. I'm so sorry! I am *so sorry*." I took a juddering breath. "I'm such a failure, a *complete* failure. I feel so bad. I'm sorry, Michael." My eyes were fiery with tears.

Michael sighed. "I was worried you were hurt."

"I *am* hurt! I'm always hurting when it comes to trich!" I tried to swallow a sob.

"Ann, I'm really sorry." His voice was steady and measured—everything I couldn't be in that moment. "But it is okay. *You* are okay. This doesn't make you a failure or a bad person. Don't worry about the money."

The tears were falling rapidly now; I brushed them away with the back of my hand, trying to keep them off the cell phone. "But it's so much money—$150! I thought this would help me! And now I look worse than I did before. And on top of that, I'm a freak! I can't stop when I want to—-I just pull again and again and again!"

My voice was louder than I'd realized; Jess had heard me and cracked open the hotel door. Her eyes were narrow slits in the hallway light.

"Are you okay?" she mouthed. There were three other girls in the room with us; I'd probably woken everyone up. She was in the barely awake stage I knew from our time together as roommates: alert but ready to fall asleep in seconds.

I shook my head and shrugged. Placing my hand over the bottom of the phone, I whispered back, "My eyelashes. Bad night. I'm talking to Michael."

Jess: the one friend I didn't have to explain anything to. I was deeply thankful for her in that moment and so grateful that she was a safe place for my heart.

"I love you," she mouthed and gently clicked the door shut.

I focused my attention back on my husband. "I want to be free of this, Michael. Every time I hope something new will work, it never does. Never! I'm just as bad as I was before, or worse. I feel like I'm never going to be free of this."

"You will be. We'll keep praying." He paused. "And Ann? You're beautiful to me."

I shook my head. "I don't feel like it."

"You are." He sighed. "Why don't we pray together and then you try to sleep? You need to rest."

I stretched out my legs and listened to the cadence of his voice, the calm timbre asking Jesus to give me peace, to heal me, to help me, to enable me to let go of any false guilt. I tried to shake the tension out of my shoulders, and then I took some deep breaths and told Michael that I loved him. He told me the same, and I hung up.

The next morning I locked the bathroom door and ran the shower while I tried to fix what was left of my real lashes and the few fake ones still remaining. They didn't look good; what I'd done to myself the night before assured that. I never felt good about how my eyes looked, but that morning was one of my all-time lows. Eyelashes are the quintessential feminine quality in a face, and I had hardly any. I wore heavy eyeliner for the wedding that day, grateful it was a formal affair.

Thankfully, no one was looking much at me anyway. The wedding was stunning, overlooking the Atlantic Ocean. Elsie was a radiant beauty, and the wedding was a picture of faith and love. I was able to genuinely celebrate her and Jeff and the marriage they were starting. Still, always lingering with me was the feeling of shame. Between the laughter and the dancing and the abundance of fresh seafood and steak (again!), I kept trying to push back the thoughts of wasting money and looking ugly. I tried to forget how much I felt like a failure.

Our Inability to Fix Ourselves

We don't know, explicitly, what role shame played in the life of the Bleeding Woman. Still, the Scriptures allude to it. In Mark's Gospel, the writer refers to her bleeding condition as a *mastix*, a vivid term related to the idea of "scourge" or "torment." One biblical scholar notes that this Greek term "combines physical suffering and shame, hence something akin to punishment."[2] The Bleeding Woman's condition put her at odds with her community since, according to the law, she was unclean. Anyone who touched her would also be unclean; anyone who even sat in the same chair she had been sitting in would be rendered unclean too. So she probably didn't leave home much, or at all. She couldn't have had a social life in any regular way.

Her waiting had been so long that the people in her town would have certainly assumed that something was amiss. Whether people knew the truth about why she had stopped coming to weekly worship or backyard picnics, they eventually understood that something was causing her to be perpetually unclean. The Bleeding Woman was an outcast in her own village, unable to participate in community life. No wonder she felt tormented and shamed.

Even her plan to come up *behind* Jesus to touch his robe, without having to face him, supports the idea that her emotional state was wounded and that perhaps she saw herself as shameful or unworthy. She didn't want to be seen, didn't want to be noticed, didn't want to be acknowledged. She simply wanted to slink up, touch his robe, and disappear.

Isn't this what shame does? Whether our struggle is physical, emotional, or spiritual, shame can feel like salt in the proverbial wound. It stings; it adds pain to the struggle we are already slogging through. Shame can push us further away from people than our original weakness ever could by making us think that we must hide, that we must not let our weakness be noticed, that we must never let our problem or sin into the light.

Shame is what kept me from telling most of my close friends about trichotillomania for years. I'm talking about my closest friends, not just acquaintances or coworkers. Even Elsie—whose wedding I traveled hundreds of miles for—knew so much of my heart, but she didn't know about trich. Why? Shame.

I couldn't tell Elsie that I had trich and that I was "working on it," the way you can tell someone that your car's transmission is broken but it's in the shop getting fixed. I had no definite end point for this problem, no way to guarantee when or if I would be free of it.

It's not that I wasn't still trying. I attempted everything I could think of to fix myself. In addition to the strategies I had tried as a kid and the one-time tries like the semipermanent false lashes, here are some things I did regularly:

1. Wore tape on my fingers
2. Wore glasses instead of contacts
3. Reapplied mascara five times a day
4. Prayed
5. Prayed again
6. Played with Silly Putty
7. Wore gloves in the house
8. Prayed some more

But nothing had healed me, and it appeared that nothing *could* heal me. When I kept arriving at that dead end, the shame started to build up, right there in the cul-de-sac of my struggle. I was constantly aware that I was broken and that I had no way—no plan or procedure—to make everything better.

In fact, it felt impossible to ever get better. *The American Journal of Psychiatry* states, "From a neurocognitive perspective, trichotillomania can be considered a habit disorder in which the sufferer is unable to exert sufficient top-down inhibitory control."[3] I was unable to "exert top-down inhibitory control." It's a plastic way of saying that I lacked self-control in this one area of my life even though I desperately wanted it. When it came to exercising, studying, and writing, self-control was no problem. But that wasn't the case with trich. In that realm, I felt completely out of control, out of my senses, tuned in to only one thing: the feeling of hair between my fingers.

Michael would ask me what I thought about when I was in the "zone" of pulling out my eyelashes. The truth was, it was the one time I didn't think about much of anything. But I always had a feeling I could name: shame.

It was the shame of knowing that what I hated came from myself.

I was ashamed to be a bearer of the condition, ashamed to be the carrier of such a strange and unknown disorder. And I was ashamed that I was the one doing it to myself. I assumed that if anyone knew what I did, their response would be the same: "You pull out your own hair? That's so weird. Just stop!"

But I couldn't. And it made me ashamed of my own hands and, at times, my own life.

What Shame Does to Us

When you're waiting—waiting for something to change, to go away, to get better, to heal, or to grow—and when that thing you're waiting for doesn't happen, shame is often willing to take its place. Shame loves to pair itself with struggle, and it loves to make us believe that it has to stay with us in the unanswered and challenging parts of our stories. The enemy wants us to believe that in the messy and difficult aspects of our lives, shame is *meant* to be there, that it's an emotion we have to own. I think that many of us are so used to letting shame live as a parasite in our place of struggle that it's hard to imagine our lives without it.

That's why I hadn't told Elsie about my struggle with trichotillomania for all the years I'd known her, even though she'd shared so much of her life with me. Although I knew Elsie as a gracious, loving, loyal friend, I was too embarrassed to tell her about trich. I was worried that it would make me seem incapable or weird.

In short, I was ashamed.

In the same way the Bleeding Woman came up behind Jesus to avoid having her shame revealed, I did all I could to keep trich in the shadows, even with a trusted friend. I didn't want her to see what a mess I was on the inside.

All those fears, all those worries about how Elsie would perceive me if she knew the truth, stemmed from shame. I worried that once others knew about my condition, they would see me differently. I didn't want them to look at me for signs of trich, for signs of my brokenness. Although I knew that Jess and Michael and my family didn't look at me differently, I wondered if they were the exception to the rule. *Besides,* I cautioned myself, *they have to love me. They're my people.*

I couldn't imagine that anyone else could see me through a lens of grace, because I couldn't see myself through a lens of grace.

That's what shame did: it twisted my understanding of reality and grace. I felt ashamed that I couldn't get it together, that I constantly struggled, that I couldn't muster up enough strength to conquer this. The shame made it seem impossible for me to accept grace for my constant failures.

I was ashamed of my own need for grace.

That's why I so rarely told my story to anyone—even to very close friends.

The Bleeding Woman was ashamed of her own need; that's why she planned to sneak up behind Jesus.

And yet. Yet.

The gospel shows us that God is not ashamed of our need:

There is therefore now no condemnation for those who are in Christ Jesus. For the law of the Spirit of life has set you free in Christ Jesus from the law of sin and death. For God has done what the law, weakened by the flesh, could not do. By sending his own Son in the likeness of sinful flesh and for sin, he condemned sin in the flesh, in order that the righteous requirement of the law might be fulfilled in us, who walk not according to the flesh but according to the Spirit.

ROMANS 8:1-4

God, it appears, has always been just fine with my extreme need and with my inability to keep everything together on my own. We so clearly need a Savior because we can't set ourselves free from sin or from death—or really from anything that entangles us. Can't keep your finances together? Can't keep your kids under control? Can't keep your grades up? Can't keep your heart nice and tidy? Can't keep your eating habits on a tight leash or your emotions buttoned up or your desires appropriate?

Neither can I.

You might not have trichotillomania. But you probably have your own places where it feels impossible to get it together. And my guess is that you have shame in those areas. You might have a hard time receiving grace amid those consistent failures and needs.

But those recurring failures and needs don't push the Lord away from us. Rather, our need—our unending, unfading, constant need for saving and for grace—is part of what drew him to our plight. *Because* we are so needy, *because* we are so incapable—that's why Jesus came, willingly and full of love, to save us.

> While we were still weak, at the right time Christ
> died for the ungodly. For one will scarcely die for a
> righteous person—though perhaps for a good person
> one would dare even to die—but God shows his love
> for us in that while we were still sinners, Christ died
> for us.
>
> ROMANS 5:6-8

He came *while we were still weak*. Not when we got our act together and overcame our struggle and sin and weakness, but while we were still weak. It has been that way all along, and it will always be that way: we are weak and broken people in need of a Savior. God knows that. He understands that. And he extends grace to us in that place, every moment of every day.

This need for sinners to have a Savior started in the Garden. Adam and Eve sinned, and then, because they were ashamed, they covered themselves (see Genesis 3:7). Nothing had changed about their bodies when they crossed over from innocence to sin—they still had the same arms and legs and ears. But the presence of sin changed their *perception* of themselves and their own nakedness. And that's when they tried to cover up who they were—*because they were ashamed.*

Shame makes it feel impossible for us to extricate ourselves from our struggles.

Shame makes it seem that our value is tied to our brokenness.

Shame pairs our worth with our weakness.

Shame yokes us to lies.

Shame tells us that our identity is only as whole as the image we can put forward.

So when I had a line of bare lashes and my image was wounded, shame told me that my identity was wounded too. When my weakness flared more than my strength, shame said that my worth was minimal, even nonexistent.

Shame is a powerful emotion. I know the power of its teeth, how it bites like a weasel, unwilling to let go.

I know how shame makes us try to cover up who we are.
Shame led me to try to cover up trich for more than a decade, to keep it a secret even when I desperately needed others on the journey with me. Shame led the Bleeding Woman to sneak up behind Jesus rather than run up to him, face to face. Shame prompts us to put up false identities and tell others that we're fine even when we're not, all because we carry the deep sense that it's not okay to not be okay.

But shame is a liar.

Culture tells us that being needy is shameful. We say it all the time in whispered tones and with looks of disdain: "She's *needy*. Watch out for her." But the truth is that being a follower of Jesus means we have acknowledged—once and for all—that we can't be okay on our own. We have owned the truth that we can't save ourselves. Being followers of Christ means not only that we believe in the gospel story but also that we are banking our lives on the fact that Jesus is the only one who is okay, the only one who has it all together, the only one who is perfect. Claiming Christ means we have thrown up our hands in surrender, admitting that we are needy in the most desperate of ways and that we are desperate for his holiness and righteousness. Only in him are we ultimately and finally okay, even when our lives are wounded and hurting and shattered.

Silencing Shame

Shame *can* be silenced. Even as we wait in unwanted realities and sickness and broken relationships, unwhole and unwell, we can still silence shame. We don't have to carry shame in the areas of our lives where we are needy and failing. We don't have to feel ashamed about the places where we are still waiting for God's touch. Even in the most staggering circumstances, shame doesn't have to have the upper hand. We know this because we see it in the life of Christ, in the most horrific of situations. The writer of Hebrews reminds us of this, recalling how Jesus lived (and died):

> Since we are surrounded by such a great cloud of witnesses, let us throw off everything that hinders and the sin that so easily entangles. And let us run with perseverance the race marked out for us, fixing our eyes on Jesus, the pioneer and perfecter of faith. For the joy set before him he endured the cross, scorning its shame, and sat down at the right hand of the throne of God. Consider him who endured such opposition from sinners, so that you will not grow weary and lose heart.
> HEBREWS 12:1-3, NIV

Knowing that a brutal death was before him, Jesus set his eyes on the joy of victory and the joy of saving his people. And he "scorned" the shame of the cross. Other translations of this passage say that Jesus "despised" the shame of the cross or "disregarded" the shame of the cross. But I love the word *scorned*, because it points me to the fact that Jesus chose—in fact, refused—to give shame the power it could have had in his life.

In Jesus' first-century culture, shame was a powerful force.

And being nailed to a cross was perhaps the most shameful thing a man could endure. Condemned as a criminal, beaten nearly senseless, and put on display in front of your enemies was a death designed to shame as much as it was designed to torture.

And still Jesus "scorned" the shame of the cross. Scorn: to refuse to give respect or approval to something; to show contempt for something; to be indignant about something; to be angry about something that is unfair or wrong. Jesus scorned the shame of the cross—he looked ahead at what was supposed to be the most shaming moment of his life, and he scorned the shame.

He took the cross, yes, but he refused to take the shame.

So why did Jesus show contempt for the shame that his culture was trying to put on him at the cross?

I think it's because Jesus knew he was enduring the horror of the cross to silence shame once and for all. He refused to accept the very shame he was dying to pay for.

Jesus died to remove our ultimate shame—the shame of being a sinful human being before a holy God. So he saw the cross not as a shaming moment in his life but as the most holy and powerful moment in history. His death—what the devil intended to bring Jesus the greatest shame—actually broke the power of shame for those who cling to the cross.

Jesus, who carried our brokenness on his shoulders and labored under the weight of our sin and shame, refused to let shame have a place in his life. He scorned it. He denied shame the respect others said it should have. He prevented shame from receiving any approval in his heart and mind.

And in doing so, he saved us from sin and from the shame we so often experience. Shame comes when something wrong has been done—by us or to us. In one way or another, all of us know the feeling of shame, because all of us have experienced wrong things in our lives. We are sinners, broken people living among broken people. That feeling of shame that leaped in me with trich— shame about how I looked and what I had done to myself, shame that I couldn't stop and sometimes didn't even want to fight the desire to pull—was real. I felt it because trich constantly reminded me that I was a broken, needy soul before the God I couldn't measure up to (see Romans 3:23). But because Jesus died for my sins, he removed all condemnation from me—he paid the price for my inability to get it together on my own. The Bible declares this powerfully:

There is therefore now no condemnation for those who are in Christ Jesus.

ROMANS 8:1

Whenever our heart condemns us, God is greater than our heart, and he knows everything.

1 JOHN 3:20

Through the Holy Spirit, we now have the power to live new lives and make new choices. Shame and condemnation no longer have to be our companions. Although we may feel shame, we, like Jesus, can choose to scorn it. We can choose to separate our identity in Christ from the ruined image we have of ourselves. We can choose to listen to the truth of Jesus and separate our worth from our weakness, our lives from lies.

Freedom from Shame

As I pursued the difficult process of removing the talons of shame from my life, I realized that it was time to finally tell Elsie I had trichotillomania. It was a tangible way, I realized, to separate my worth from my weakness.

It took me more years to call her than I want to admit, but I knew that I needed to scorn shame, and I wanted to be honest with her. This was a friend I loved and treasured, one who had shared so much of her life openly and graciously with me, and I owed her the truth. I was ready to silence the shame of trich in my life. I was ready to accept how much I needed grace from God—and from her.

I picked up the phone, knowing that this call would come out of the blue for her; she could have no idea what I was going to say.

We chatted for a bit, and then I dove in headfirst. "Elsie? I really value our friendship, and I want to tell you about this condition I've had." I went on to explain trichotillomania, how it manifested in my life and how I'd developed it in childhood.

She was mostly quiet on the other end. I wished I could see her face, wished I could have told her across a coffee table instead of across hundreds of miles.

And then I said the words I'd really called to say—the words I'd needed to say for years: "More than explaining trich to you, Elsie, I want to tell you how sorry I am that I hid this from you for so long. I'm sorry I didn't open up this part of my life to you sooner."

"Oh, Ann." I heard her voice crack. "I'm not upset. But my heart aches that I didn't know. I grieve that I couldn't walk with you through this trial, because you've walked with me through my valleys."

I was crying now too, perhaps finally feeling the cost of not being open with her about this part of my life. The cost wasn't just for me, I realized. It had cost Elsie, too. I had let shame silence me, and it had kept me from letting Elsie into my life.

"But I'm so thankful you've told me now, Ann." I heard her exhale. "We're all broken."

I nodded gratefully into the phone. She was extending such grace to me.

We *are* all broken, as Elsie reminded me. And although we may never be free from our weakness, our brokenness, or our sin—although we may continue to wait for God to change our circumstances and our hearts and our minds on this side of heaven—our identity is not in those weak and waiting places. Our identity is not in our ability to overcome; it is in Christ and his victory over death. Our identity is in his overcoming of shame and the grave. We are his. I am his. You are his.

Trich, divorce, pain, sorrow, depression, anger, fear, abuse, eating disorders, debt, wayward children, comparison, hurt: we will have struggles, but we don't have to walk in shame. I don't have to live in that shame. You don't have to live in that shame. In the truest sense, our shame is gone. Shame is defeated because our lives are hidden in Christ with God (see Colossians 3:3). To live in freedom, we have to work against shame by opening our hearts and our lives to those who love us, inviting them to extend the grace we all need from one another.

Because as we hear love and acceptance from them and from the Lord, we start to grasp the truth of the gospel for the tender and waiting places of our souls. We are not our struggles or our sins or our weaknesses. We belong to Christ. And that is all that we need to be.

CHAPTER 7

When Waiting
Feels Like Suffering

*S*arah ducked under the frame of the entrance to their family
home. The morning sun was bright in her eyes, reminding her
that she had not been outside in months. She draped a shawl over
her head and kept her eyes down. Although she was covered from
her head to her sandaled feet, she still felt exposed.

Sarah began walking, not knowing where she was going. But
she knew whom she was looking for: Jesus. Lydia had said he was
nearby, and Sarah had eked out a prayer in the dark of the night,
asking God to direct her to the healer. Now she could only hope
God heard that one prayer in all of her broken life.

Weaving her way through the streets, Sarah avoided the city gate,
where her father would be talking with other men. She turned before
reaching the house where her mother had gone to visit a friend; she

hoped her mother would linger for another hour so Sarah's absence at home could go unnoticed.

As Sarah inched closer to the heart of the small village, near the shore where the fishermen did their selling and their mending, she heard voices. There were many voices fighting for attention, but one of them was urgent. He was yelling something into the crowd.

Sarah edged closer and heard the desperate voice of Jairus. He was one of the synagogue leaders and a trusted friend of her father's. Although she had not seen him in well over a decade—a holy man could never enter the house where an unclean woman lived—she remembered his voice well. It was deep and sounded as if it had been rubbed over the hull of a fishing boat—a voice that crackled, nearly breaking into pieces with every word. Sarah joined the periphery of the crowd, trying to blend in. But no one was paying attention to her anyway.

"Rabbi!" Jairus was close to screaming, his voice tighter than Sarah had ever heard it. "Rabbi, please come with me! My little girl is next to death. It hovers at our door! Come and lay your hands on her so she may live!"

Tabitha? Tabitha was young, born around the same time Sarah started bleeding; she had never gotten to meet her. Tabitha could only be eleven or twelve. Oh, she is much too young to die! Sarah's heart wrenched within her, and she strained to get a glimpse of what was happening. She could not see any faces, but the crowd seemed to be gathered around Jairus and another man. All at once Sarah knew: it was Jesus.

And as the crowd moved to follow the two men, she was able to catch a glimpse of Jesus' face.

Sarah's breath lodged in her throat.

Because even from a distance, she could see something in his eyes she did not expect: compassion.

Something inside Sarah came undone when she saw Jesus' eyes. In a single moment, the pain of the last twelve years came rushing through her—rushing like a wind she could not see or stop. The shame, the sorrow, the disappointment, the anger. And the loneliness.

More than the constant exhaustion, more than the light-headedness, more than the intermittent ringing in her ears, what had pained her most was the inescapable loneliness she shouldered every morning. It moved with her, an unseen weight slung like a yoke around her neck. This was the hardest kind of suffering, this suffering that came not from her body but from her spirit.

The physical suffering was enough, Sarah knew. But this weight around her soul felt impossible to carry. It was a suffering that renewed itself every sunrise, when the reality of her life swallowed her as the dreams dissipated.

She had faced so many years of quiet suffering, so many years of feeling unknown and unloved. She wanted desperately to be done with it.

Sarah began to move. She had to get to Jesus.

In those years between graduating from college and having my daughter, there was one afternoon when I was reading and my struggle with trich seemed especially debilitating. I couldn't stop pulling out more eyelashes, and what bubbled out of me wasn't frustration or sorrow—it was hurt.

I was twenty-seven years old. I desperately wanted to be free from the insatiable urge to pull out my eyelashes, but I was too weak to overcome it with sheer willpower. With each eyelash I pulled out, I stumbled back into my own internal war. I knew, down deep, that I couldn't heal myself, and I also knew that God wasn't healing me.

That day it all came out—not in pretty faith, but in hot tears and screams. I sat on the couch, attempting to have a yelling match with God.

"I will never look normal, God! I feel so ugly!"

My voice rebounded off the walls.

"Thanks to trich, I haven't felt beautiful for most of my life! Why do I have this? Why?"

I was met with silence.

"God, why? *Why?* I'm living my life for you—and I've done everything I can to be free of this, but nothing works!"

I was sobbing now. I flung my book onto the tiled floor of our living room and listened to it slide across the floor.

"You know that this is the one thing I want to stop! And I can't do it on my own! Why won't you help me?"

I stood up and started pacing, my heels hitting the floor with force enough to bruise them.

"You made me to be a writer and a reader, and my trich is worst when I do these things! I can't stop it, and I hate myself for it! I hate that I'm so incapable!"

I was burning inside, the heat radiating into my fingertips. All I could do was ball my hands into fists and scream louder.

"And I hate that you could take this away in a moment, and you haven't!"

The heaving started. "I have asked and begged, and you still haven't taken this away!"

I sank to my knees. "I want you to just take it away! *Please.* I'm so tired of this. I've had trich for more years than I've been free."

I opened my hands and let the tears stream down. The exhaustion in my heart flooded into my body.

"Please free me, Lord. It's been sixteen years. My heart is so tired."

Should We Just "Get Over It"?

Those years in my mid-twenties were full of study: reading, writing, thinking, teaching, and then doing it all again. After finishing a master's degree in writing, I taught in the English department at my alma mater as an adjunct instructor, and I found that I loved teaching. I loved the dance of question and discussion, loved the curiosity of the students, loved the topics we wrote about. So I returned to graduate school to complete my master of fine arts in writing and spent another handful of years studying, reading, and writing.

My MFA program was low residency, so while I was a full-time student, I still held a job as an office assistant and spent my nights and weekends writing. Twice a year, I flew across the country to take intensive classes and then headed back home to work and write some more. I turned in a new batch of written work to my professor through e-mail every three weeks, and I found that I thrived in the mix of intense coursework and thoughtful writing at home.

It was a rich season for me; I was learning how to write not as a hobby but as my profession. I read books that challenged me to go deeper in my craft and my ability. I rubbed elbows with other students who also loved writing. And I learned how to create space in my words for others to inhabit and understand. I loved it.

But I hated it too; I hated that the thing I loved, this thing I felt called to do, linked arms with the weakest part of me. That was perhaps the reason for my deepest suffering: everything I wanted to do with my life was bound up with trich. And I was exhausted from fighting a losing battle every day for sixteen years.

Perhaps the Trichotillomania Learning Center explains it best:

> One of the most destructive consequences of compulsive hair pulling is the prolonged experience of loss of control over one's own actions. The puller not only feels like the victim of an irrational, destructive act, but like the perpetrator of it as well. It is as if one has become a battleground for a horrible and out-of-control struggle. Eventually there develops a sense of oneself as a helpless and exhausted witness to this endlessly repeating trauma.[1]

And it was "endlessly repeating." I pulled out my eyelashes the most when I was reading or studying or typing. When my hands were busy—when I was working out or making dinner or having coffee with a friend, my hands ringing the paper cup—I didn't pull. When I lectured to my students with a dry erase marker in my hand, or when I was out to dinner with my husband and friends, I didn't think about my lashes. But when I sat in a quiet space with a book or a laptop computer, or when I sat at my desk with a stack of papers to grade, I would compulsively pull out my eyelashes. The desire to feel lashes between my fingers blazed when I was doing what I loved most and best.

My purpose in life, I knew, was bound up in loving Jesus and others, and also in my work as a writer and a teacher. I spent hours every week in front of a computer screen, releasing words onto digital pages. I read. I drank the words of others so I could learn and grow, and I wrote feedback for the budding writers who were in my classes. Yet those were the places where I struggled with trich the most.

Sitting down to write an article—something I loved doing—also meant that I would probably get out of my chair with fewer lashes than I had before. Either that or I would spend an inordinate amount of time trying *not* to pull out my eyelashes, wasting the time I should have spent writing. I could never just sit down at my computer without doing the one thing I hated. I'd been pulling out my lashes for fourteen, fifteen, sixteen years, and by now the suffering wasn't just from trich. After all this time, the waiting itself felt like suffering.

If I couldn't get away from trich, why hadn't God given me different passions, ones that didn't tie me up with constant opportunities for trich to worsen? Why, instead of creating me to love writing, couldn't he have made me to love surgery or swimming or softball—something that would keep my hands busy and occupied? I constantly felt like what I was called to do was stained by my own struggle. My deepest joys were scattered in a personal minefield of failure and disappointment.

Still, I hesitate to even use the word *suffer* in relation to my experience with trich. It's a word with such broad scope, and it seems inadequate to pair the pain I experienced with the tragedies that strike all around the world. Turn on the news, and you'll see it well enough through pixels; travel any distance, and you'll smell it up close.

I have seen deep suffering. When my husband and I traveled with a team from our church to South Africa to help a sister church near Cape Town, I saw suffering of a magnitude I'd never imagined.

Cape Town is undoubtedly the most stunning place my feet have ever stepped on. The oceans foam from light green to deep blue, and the mountains surge from those oceans like hands lifted in praise. I was in South Africa only ten days, and I spent one of those days seaside, trying to memorize the water that surprised me with its clarity and beauty. The other nine days were spent in Masiphumelele, a township birthed out of the apartheid that began in the country in 1948. Apartheid: a time when entire people groups were shoved into walled cities based on their skin color, and ghettos were imposed due to racism.

Masiphumelele is one of those townships. Although

apartheid technically no longer exists, its thorns remain. Generations of poverty produce generations of poverty, and for most people born into these walled slums, there's no way out.

Bits of the original wall still surround Masiphumelele, but today the walls that lock people inside are made of something other than cement or brick. Roughly thirty thousand people live in an area that is less than a mile wide. More than 20 percent of those living in the township are HIV positive, and tuberculosis is rampant. Unemployment hovers around 70 percent.[2]

Yes, I saw suffering there. I became friends with Fereka, who was HIV positive, seven months pregnant, and married to an alcoholic. She lived in a rented shack made of cardboard and tin—they couldn't afford to buy it. And there was Jasmine, the sweet teenager who became my sidekick and my sister, who wore the same shirt for the nine days I saw her. She had no way out of the poverty that surrounded her, no options available.

As I got to know and love and pray with these women, I felt deeply grieved by my richness and my privilege and my options. I felt ashamed that I'd spent more money to get to their slum than most of them would make in a year. Was my presence really necessary? Of course not. Was I? Hardly. I wondered if I should have stayed home and wired my dollars to our sister church so they could be turned into rands (the local currency) and used for something more than my feeble presence and tearful prayers.

I felt like I didn't help at all. But the women there who

loved me—and whom I loved in return—told me that I was changing things simply by loving and being present. I told them that their love was changing me, too. In the midst of great suffering, Jasmine's quick-hearted response to believe in Jesus and Fereka's hope for the child in her womb reflected the love of Christ. I saw resilience and determination in their response to him and to their circumstances, and it marked me. While I couldn't offer them much, I knew they were not alone; they were now connected with the church in Masiphumelele, which was doing the beautiful and hard work of helping to change the infrastructure of the town.

We left, of course; we went back to our homes made of wood and brick, to our lives full of opportunities that would have been unfathomable to the women I came to love in Masiphumelele. And although I was in South Africa for only ten days, the memories come back to me often. They blur with memories from my time in Honduras and Mexico, where many men and women I met—and love—live in poverty and pain. They blur with memories of walking along the river in Chicago, where homeless men and women beg for money and food.

Sometimes when I think of those memories or when I watch the news or read the paper, the suffering of the world feels unbearable. I can't bear to feel it all at once, lest I crumble in front of the screen or faint between the folds of paper. Letting myself engage with the suffering of others can feel like a burden that's too heavy to bear.

So how dare I name trichotillomania as suffering? After

returning from South Africa, I remember feeling ridiculous about my struggle with trich. It felt even more absurd to pray to God, begging him for freedom from a condition that didn't kill me or even hurt me in any physical way. I realized that I had prayed for my own freedom from this condition more than I'd prayed for the freedom of sex slaves or for food for those dying from starvation. I felt ludicrous, selfish, silly.

I berated my heart for caring so much about something so small in the eyes of the world. When I thought about the suffering in the world, even the suffering I'd seen with my own eyes, I felt small and self-centered. Was I foolish for daring to call what I experienced with trichotillomania suffering?

For a while, my prayers for healing from trich were laced with guilt, and I tried to make up for it by praying for others who were suffering differently than I was—for Fereka and Jasmine and the millions of children around the world without parents or food or comfort.

It made me pause and ponder: Should I just get over trichotillomania? Should I just hurdle it and move on? Maybe I should stop praying about it, stop thinking about it, stop being concerned about the way it filled the porous and tender places in my mind. Should I just put on my big girl pants and act as if everything were fine?

I don't think so. I don't think that's what Jesus was asking of me.

Here's why: the story of the Bleeding Woman.

Acknowledging the Pain

In that season of feeling defeated by trich, I circled back to the Bleeding Woman—this generous woman whose story has been told for so long. And I started writing about her.

Her story had always resonated with me, so while I was in my master of fine arts (MFA) program, I wrote an essay about her. I wrote about trich in the essay too; I found that it was the beating heart of the story, the place where my life intersected with hers. But up until then, I had never written about trich anywhere other than in my personal journal.

In those earlier years, it felt too hard to write about trichotillomania, too raw. But the longer I lived with the condition, the more I realized that I wanted to write about it. I wanted to try to do what I did with everything else in my life: unravel my thoughts on the page through words.

After I had written the essay, I debated about turning it in. The professor who would read and critique my work was a writing hero of mine—a woman who wrote gorgeous prose and could turn phrases like keys in well-oiled locks. And I was back to where I'd been before: I didn't want another person—my professor, of all people—to think I was strange.

But deadlines in graduate school are real things, and I had nothing else of substance to offer to my professor. So I sent in the essay. And I waited.

She sent back encouraging words about the structure of the piece and the quality of the prose, and offered constructive criticism in the weak places of the text. But she said very little about the subject matter of trichotillomania. I wasn't sure what to think.

Not long after that, it was time for an intensive week of class, so I flew out to the West Coast for a week of writing, words, and lectures. I was scheduled to meet with my professor twice during the week, and the moment when she and I sat down to discuss my work from the previous months is sealed in my memory. We met in the cottage where she was living for the week, and the living area was all softness and large chairs; there wasn't a hard piece of furniture to be found. After she poured me a warm drink, we sat together at opposite ends of the pale green couch, my work a stack of papers between us.

My professor stretched her arm over the back of the couch and took a long look at me. She had intimidated me before I got to know her; she's fiercely intelligent and says what she means. But I had also learned that she laughs easily, and well.

"Ann. This condition that you have—trich? Is that how you say it?"

I nodded, then crossed my legs. It sounds like *trick*, and she had pronounced it correctly.

"Ann, this sounds awful. How do you deal with it?" Her glasses caught the afternoon light coming in through the windows.

"I don't know. I mean, it's just normal for me now. I don't like it, obviously. I hate it. But it's what I know; it's what I live with."

She picked up the essay and flipped from the first page to the second. "Well, I'm sorry that you do. It sounds like a very difficult condition to have."

My professor wasn't emotional. She wasn't saccharine. She

didn't pity me. But I felt her compassion that afternoon, the way she reached out in kindness. She acknowledged that I was suffering.

It was her acknowledgment of the suffering that was a gift to me that day. She didn't ignore my struggle with trich or act as if it were something to be danced around. But neither did she blow it out of proportion and let it overtake our conversation. She recognized it for what it was in my life and let it be what it was to me—no more, no less. Because of that, I felt secure in her acknowledgment and her kindness, able to talk about the essay with her candidly. More than anything, I felt seen and known on that green couch. She wanted to understand me, both as a person and as a writer.

Studying the story of the Bleeding Woman helped me to better understand the reality of suffering and that Jesus wasn't asking me to ignore my struggle with trich. Here's why: just as my professor offered me an extension of grace on the couch that afternoon, Jesus offered a similar—and better—response to the Bleeding Woman. He didn't minimize her suffering; he didn't suggest that she toughen up. Instead, he validated her pain.

Before we can appreciate why his response is so powerful, however, we must first understand what is actually taking place in this story. In the Gospel of Mark, the story of the Bleeding Woman is paired like a turtledove with the story of Jairus's daughter—the twelve-year-old girl Jesus raised from the dead:

When Jesus had crossed again in the boat to the other side, a great crowd gathered about him, and he was beside the sea. Then came one of the rulers of the synagogue, Jairus by name, and seeing him, he fell at his feet and implored him earnestly, saying, "My little daughter is at the point of death. Come and lay your hands on her, so that she may be made well and live." And he went with him.

MARK 5:21-24

Jesus went with Jairus on an errand of eternal importance. Now that I'm a mother, I can see my husband's face in Jairus's. Had it been our daughter, Ella, on that bed, hanging in the space between life and death, Michael would have been running down the streets with panic written in his eyes, with fear flaming his muscles, with hope causing the hair on his arms to stand at electric attention. This was a father with one chance left. He would have looked like a crazy man—crazy in love with his little girl, desperate for her healing. Desperate for a miracle. Running, running; searching, searching for the man they said could heal. I don't think words are enough to do this father's love justice. "He fell at his feet and implored him earnestly," Mark tells us.

But picture it today. See that father running the streets of downtown Chicago, see him coming upon a crowd gathered around Jesus, and see him flinging himself in front of the rabbi. Hear the break in his voice as the question tumbles out of his mouth: "Will you come? Please, *please* come!"

And Jesus said yes. Perhaps those in the crowd nodded

their heads. Jairus was known—he was a leader, a ruler—surely Jesus would help other leaders like himself. Then he took to the streets with Jairus, heading to the house that held the dying little girl. And Jairus allowed himself to hope.

Here in this Scripture account, Jairus has a name, Jairus has a title, and Jairus receives a response from Jesus.

But then from the back of the crowd comes the Bleeding Woman. We never hear her name, although Jesus—the one who is God and man, the one who counts the stars and knows them all by name—surely knew it. He knew her story, too. But she didn't want to be seen; all she wanted to do was touch his robe and slip away.

Although there is so much to this story—other beautiful and wonderful things—what matters to me here is that *Jesus acknowledged her suffering.* We can't miss this. We dare not miss this. What the Bleeding Woman didn't know when she made the decision to touch his robe was that Jesus would stop the thronging procession just for her, even though there was a little girl who was dying down the street.

Death was coming like a flame toward a girl who couldn't run from it. There was agony in Jairus's eyes—*Hurry, hurry! Please!*—and yet Jesus stopped for the Bleeding Woman. Her suffering was not, in the world's eyes, nearly as important. It was hardly urgent, as she'd been living with this condition for well over a decade. It seemed she could continue to live, bleeding indefinitely. Death wasn't knocking at her proverbial door.

The crowd could understand Jairus's urgency. But no one would have felt urgency on behalf of the Bleeding Woman.

The people in her own town most likely knew her story and counted her as invisible, dead as she was to communal worship and celebration. They wouldn't have stopped for her, wouldn't have acknowledged her. "Why not attend to her later?" we can almost hear those around Jairus say. Surely the suffering of the Bleeding Woman wasn't as important as that of the little girl about to be dropped from life into death.

But.

But her suffering was significant to Jesus. He understood that her waiting had been part of her suffering—that the waiting itself had *caused* her suffering. And that suffering mattered to him. It mattered enough that he was willing to stop the leader of the synagogue—the one with the name and the prestige—and give his full attention, time, and love to a woman too poor to pay for one more doctor's visit.

Jesus validated her suffering by stopping for her, by seeking her out. She wasn't any less worthy of his attention because her suffering was less immediate or less dire than that of Jairus's daughter. He didn't tell her to come back later or that he was attending to more important matters. In the face of another person's death, in fact, he affirmed her search for healing and her faith in his ability to do so.

Only Jesus can hold things like this in tandem. Only Jesus can simultaneously attend to the one with the broken foot and the one with stage IV cancer. Only Jesus can concurrently care about the child withering away from starvation and the child weeping over his parents' divorce. Only Jesus can cry with the girl sobbing over a high school breakup and the wife who is widowed, left with mouths to feed and an empty bed. He is the only one who can see that all pain is real and valid, regardless of how the world would rank it. He is the only one who can validate our suffering—*and he does.*

The pain of the Bleeding Woman was legitimate, and the Maker of the universe knew what her suffering had cost her. Her cost may not have come through searing pain—although the Scriptures don't tell us one way or the other. Her pain may have come through social stigmas that no one else understood. It may have come through a loneliness so great she felt the weight of it like marble blocks on her shoulders. It may have come through the exhaustion of still not being healed, the daily reminder of her own impurity and "otherness" from those around her. It may have come as a result of waiting for a breakthrough that felt impossible.

Jesus saw my struggle with trichotillomania, and he knew what it cost me. He knew how it wore me down with its incessancy. He understood that it chipped away at how I saw myself as someone made in his image, how it made me question if my prayers mattered.

Jesus doesn't negate our suffering because it is different from the pain someone else may be facing. He is just as attentive and present to the new mother suffering from postpartum depression in a million-dollar house as he is to the mother who has an alcoholic husband and is dying of AIDS in a South African shantytown. Jesus knows the suffering that each of us carries, and he knows the genuine pain and sorrow in every heart. He knows that sometimes the years of unending struggle and suffering are themselves too heavy to bear.

He knows. And he cares. He is a present and loving Savior. He sees you, and he understands your suffering. He knows the pain you've walked through and the days when it all seems impossible and you can barely put one foot in front of the other.

You keep track of all my sorrows.
You have collected all my tears in your bottle.
You have recorded each one in your book.
PSALM 56:8, NLT

God understands. Not one tear has been lost on him. Not a single one. Your suffering is as real to him as it has been to you. He knows what it has cost you, and he wants to comfort you in your pain.

Pain as an Idol
Before we move on to the rest of the Bleeding Woman's encounter with Jesus, there is one more thing we must notice about her. She wasn't the one who declared her suffering. She didn't run into the crowd, bemoaning her condition, making herself the center of attention. She didn't put herself on center stage for the events that took place on the way to Jairus's house. In fact, she wanted to sneak up behind Jesus, receive her healing, and slink away. She wasn't yelling at him or making demands of him. She ran to Jesus without

an introduction, believing that he could offer her what she needed. And he did.

This is the flip side of the suffering that the Bleeding Woman experienced. She was suffering greatly, yes, but that wasn't her focus when she approached Jesus. She cared more about getting close to Jesus than about making sure he knew how much she'd suffered. The goal, for her, was reaching Jesus.

Although Jesus deeply affirms our suffering, and although he catches each tear and profoundly understands every trial we have walked through, the suffering isn't meant to be the focus of our lives. Jesus must be the focus. Anytime we take Jesus' affirmation of our suffering as carte blanche to worship our pain rather than him, we've missed the point.

I know I've done this before. I wince when I think about it, but it's true. At times, my suffering came to feel bigger than anything else in my life. A sense of twisted self-pity would sweep in, and I'd find myself thinking that trich was *my* struggle, *my* cross to bear, *my* pain. And when I let it, trich threatened to unseat God in his place of authority and rule in my life. In a backward way, I have sometimes made an idol of my suffering by letting it be the biggest thing in my mind and in my heart.

There were so many times when Michael and I went around the same trich mountain, with me refusing to see any way out of my pain. And there was one night when he called me out.

"I feel so ugly," I whispered, my head on his chest. "And I hate what I'm doing to myself." We were sitting on the

ANN SWINDELL

taupe couch in our living room, the gray tile cold beneath my feet.

He kissed the top of my head. "You're not ugly, Ann. You are a beautiful woman, and I love you."

"But I can never stop."

Michael leaned his cheek against my head and tightened his arm around mine.

"So we keep praying, and we do the things we know to do."

I couldn't hear him; I didn't want to. I was zoned in on my struggle, my pain, my hurt. "I don't have much hope left that this will ever change. It hasn't changed for so long, so why would it ever get better?"

Michael didn't respond. He just held me.

I whispered the question I needed him to answer: "Do you have hope for me?"

Michael paused. "I believe that you will be healed, Ann. I don't know when or how, but I have hope for you. There's always hope with Jesus." He pulled away from me to look me in the face. His eyes searched mine, and when he spoke, his voice was firm. "Do you want to be healed?"

"Of course!" I shot back, my voice louder than I expected. He knew how desperately I wanted to be healed. Why would he ask that? My ears were hot. "That's not a fair question."

"Yes, it is. Because if you want to be healed, you have to stop the way you're thinking."

I looked away.

"I love you, Ann, and I always see you as beautiful. That has never changed. But if you want to see *yourself* differently

159

and if you want to walk in freedom, you have to change your thoughts. If you keep focusing on how you feel about trich, it's not going to help. You need to focus on Jesus. You need to focus on the truth of his Word."

The words stung, but they resonated in the place of deep pain that had been building over the months and years.

"Whether or not Jesus heals you, the only way out of the pit you're in is to focus on him. You can't let your struggle with trich be the deciding factor in your life." Michael paused. "If you do, it will eat you up."

I didn't have to worship my pain with hymns and praise to let it be the driving force in my life. I just had to let it uproot God as the central focus.

I took a deep breath and let it out in a rush. I sat with his words for one minute, then two. I needed courage and humility to say that he was right; it took me a couple minutes to find both.

"You're right." I paused. "I know you're right. And I'm sorry."

The Center of Our Story

When we start seeing our pain and suffering and the struggles we endure as the high pitch of our experience, or when we start demanding that God heal us, or when we make the end of suffering the goal of our relationship with him, we have put our suffering above Jesus. This happens when we start making ourselves and our suffering the center of the story we're living, regardless of what that suffering is.

There were years when I did that with trich. It wasn't that

my struggle wasn't real; it was. But when I started to put the pain above Jesus in my heart and mind, then my suffering took the throne. And when that happened, suffering became the idol I worshiped.

My suffering became the focus, and therefore *I* became the focus.

This story we're living wasn't intended to have us in the middle of it. There is one sun in this system, one Son everything else revolves around, and his name is "the bright morning star" (Revelation 22:16). We are not the center of this story. He is. But still, it's hard to live in the tension of letting Jesus acknowledge and affirm our suffering without allowing the suffering itself to become the focus. It can feel like a teeter-totter, constantly tipping toward one extreme or the other. So how do we faithfully acknowledge the reality of pain while not letting the pain hold the central place in our lives? How do we keep from idolizing our suffering?

This is the only method I've found: to avoid navel-gazing, we must practice Christ-gazing. We must focus on the one who knows suffering. The prophet Isaiah declares,

Surely he took up our pain
and bore our suffering.

ISAIAH 53:4, NIV

Jesus not only understands suffering—he bore it. He has already experienced it. Jesus can affirm our suffering because *he has suffered it with us.* The focus no longer needs to be on the suffering but on the King who carried it and who already paid the cost for it all. Someone had to pay for all this suffering. The suffering of millions—including the suffering of trichotillomania, the suffering the Bleeding Woman carried in her veins—has all been paid for. Jesus can attend intimately to each one, with true love and compassion, because he knows each one. The shame I wrestled with? He paid for it on the cross. The weakness the Bleeding Woman wore like a cloak for twelve years? He paid for it on the cross.

The story of the Bleeding Woman, although it's in part an acknowledgment of her suffering, ultimately points back to Jesus. This, I think, is what suffering is meant to do—to point us first to the suffering Christ and then, ultimately, to point us to the resurrected Christ.

Jesus suffered greatly, and then he was resurrected with a new body and with hope for all people. He still bears scars—a reminder of his own suffering—but he is the glorified one. And when my own suffering and pain threaten to usurp the place of Christ in my life, I have to choose to turn my eyes back to the cross and the empty tomb. There I remember that he suffered more than anyone. The one who understands my suffering also lived through it—and now lives victoriously.

In him, we live victoriously as well. Victory may not look the way we expect; it may not be full victory today. But this is what we're promised as his beloved.

Our suffering here isn't the end of the story. It's part of our stories, but it doesn't have the final word. Jesus does. And that is good news indeed.

CHAPTER 8

When Waiting Is Risky

*S*arah had to get to Jesus.

She moved into the crowd, holding her head covering securely under her chin. Her right hand was free; she would need it if she managed to reach Jesus.

Threading her way through the throng of people, Sarah kept her eyes down and her shoulders hunched. She was in the thick of the crowd now, just a few yards behind the rabbi. It is now or never, *Sarah thought.* If he does not heal me now, I will forever be bleeding and alone.

But even as she kept moving her feet with the crowd that pulsed around Jesus, everything inside her seemed to freeze in place. The risk she was taking was enormous, she knew that.[1] The fear that she would make the rabbi unclean and bear the consequences of that sin clamored inside her. A voice in her head screamed that this was futile, like everything else she had tried. Every concoction she had drunk, every sacrifice she had made—nothing had worked! Why would this?

But then she saw Jesus walk by. His eyes held compassion and an unnerving strength—a strength she had never seen in any other man.

Maybe he really was the Messiah. Maybe the rumors were true. Maybe he could heal her.

Yes, her heart whispered. *He can heal me. Hope pitched within her, and she rode it like a foaming wave in the sea.*

I believe. I believe he can heal me.

Sarah wove past two more men until she was directly behind Jesus. She was being nudged and jostled on all sides, and she knew that the longer she stayed, the more people she would make unclean. They might not know it, but she did, and she fought back the guilt even there in the crowd. My very life brings harm to everyone.

But she could not focus on her failures again; she had only a moment, and she knew what she must do. She could see the tassels hanging from his garment, and she recalled the words she had heard read aloud in the synagogue before her bleeding started:

The LORD said to Moses, "Speak to the people of Israel, and tell them to make tassels on the corners of their garments throughout their generations, and to put a cord of blue on the tassel of each corner. And it shall be a tassel for you to look at and remember all the commandments of the LORD, to do them."

NUMBERS 15:37-39

The tassel: a sign of God's law, a sign of the rabbi's authority.[2]

She was directly behind Jesus now. And there, in the middle of the crowd, Sarah reached down, dropped to her knees, and grasped the tassel dangling from Jesus' hem.

For a breath, she held the thread in her hands. It was thin, a whisper between her fingers.

Sarah let go.

She knelt, unmoving. Mercifully, the crowd passed by without crushing her. And there on the ground, her shawl dripping in dust, Sarah felt it.

She knew.

She was healed.

I wish I could tell this part of my story differently. Really, I do.

Because here is where my story diverges from the account in the Gospels.

The Bleeding Woman was healed. I am not.

I still have trichotillomania.

Day in and day out, for more years than I want to remember, I have been a bearer of this condition, this diagnosis. I haven't yet had my healing moment with Jesus. I haven't yet had my prayers answered in the way I dream about.

Every day, and sometimes every hour, I struggle with trich. I'm a woman still in need of healing. This side of heaven, I may always be. I don't know.

Unlike the Bleeding Woman, I don't yet have a similar miracle to report. Her story gives me hope, but it's not my own. And so, while I may not have waded into a physical crowd of people, this book—even the writing of it—is my risk. And like the Bleeding Woman, I have walked into this venture with great fear: fear that every person I touch with this book will glance at me differently, hesitantly. Like her, I'm stepping into a great throng of people, and I don't know how things will turn out.

I worry that in telling my story, I will open new doors to my shame and fear—doors I've now been trying to slam for more than two decades. To tell you the truth, after keeping trichotillomania private for so long, signing the contract to write this book felt like one of the riskiest things I've ever done.

Faith Is Spelled "R-I-S-K"

For the past twenty years, only a handful of family members and friends have known about my struggle with trich. I rarely shared about my condition with others, and when I did, it was because I'd known them as safe people for years, if not for decades. My fear cornered me into believing I needed to have a lot of social currency with someone before taking the risk of telling them about trich.

Writing this book has forced me to live inversely. I started writing not knowing if it would be published, but I wrote all the same—in the quiet of libraries and the hum of coffee shops. I directed my heart and my pen toward the Lord, meeting him as I unraveled the pain and healing that trich had brought about in my journey with him.

After writing in solitude for years, I felt the Lord nudge

my heart: it was time to send this book out. I hesitated, knowing that would mean pitching the book to agents and editors and publishing houses, to teams of people I didn't know and didn't trust. Strangers would be reading about my life and my condition. It felt risky, putting my story in the hands of people who may or may not understand, who may or may not treat me kindly, who may or may not think me strange.

I couldn't spend decades determining if a publishing team would be trustworthy or kind or safe enough to hand over my book to. When I sent the proposal out, it went out on its own. The pages and ink went ahead of me and spoke for me; I didn't know where my words would land.

But those words did land, along with a book contract— and then so did the questions. Friends and acquaintances were thrilled for me: "A book contract! Your first book! What is it about?" I usually mentioned something about the Bleeding Woman's story, intentionally ignoring my own. Later, when I was in the middle of writing this book, our family moved to a new state, where we started a new chapter of life. I was constantly meeting new people, and they inevitably asked about my work. This book was my work, so I had to make some choices.

At my first coffee date with our new pastor's wife, I wondered if the question would come up. It did—within the first five minutes. We were in the corner coffee shop in the business district, sitting near the windows that overlooked the metered parking.

Rebekah slid into her seat with a latte in hand. I had

gotten there a few minutes earlier and had already started sipping my coffee.

"So your husband told me that you're a writer!" Rebekah said.

"I am." I forced a smile, sensing the direction this was going.

"What do you write about?" She lifted the latte to her lips, waiting for me to speak.

"Well, I write for various publications about faith and how we can encounter God in the midst of our everyday lives. I'm working on a book right now too."

"Wow! A book—what's it about?"

I tugged at the edge of the brown sleeve on my cup, tearing the cardboard away from the glue holding it together.

I had a choice, there in the coffee shop: to tell the truth or to hide it. I'd been circumventing this question in some form for most of my life, trying to wriggle out of explaining trichotillomania. Even when my book came up in conversation, I'd been doing all I could to dodge the question.

As I sat there with the coffee cup sleeve in front of me, I thought, *How long? How long can I hide this? Until the book comes out and then she reads it on her own?*

No. There in the coffee shop with Rebekah, something in my soul shifted, and I made my choice. No more hiding.

I took a deep breath. "Well, it's a book about the Bleeding Woman from Scripture, and it's also about my journey with a condition called trichotillomania. Have you heard of it?"

Rebekah shook her head slightly.

"It's a condition where people pull out their hair, and

they can't stop. In my case, I pull out my eyelashes and eyebrows, but some people pull out hair from their heads, their arms—everywhere."

Rebekah hadn't taken her eyes off mine. "That sounds really hard, Ann. I'm so sorry."

She paused, and I didn't know what to say.

"How long have you had this?" she asked.

"Since I was eleven. It's been over twenty years now."

"I feel like I've heard about it, but never with that name."

Her eyes were soft, her brow wrinkled in concern and kindness.

"You might have. It's more common than you might imagine."

"So how are you tying your story and hers together?"

The tightness in my stomach loosened, and I realized that I'd been waiting for her to recoil. Instead, she extended kindness—and I took it. I took her kindness and told her about the book, which led to telling her more of my story. When I was out of words, I turned the conversation to her. Rebekah opened up and told me about how she had come to know Jesus years before.

Our time together was easy, even refreshing. But days afterward, I found myself wondering what she thought of me. Had I ruined that first impression—the one that's impossible to get back—by telling her about trich? Was she just acting nice but would later go home and tell her husband how strange the new church member was?

Call me silly, but no matter how long I've had trich, it still feels like a risk, every single time, to tell my story. I've been hiding this condition for most of my life, so bringing it into the light, whether on the page or from my own tongue, feels like betraying an unspoken pact I made with myself years ago. It's a risk, telling others about my brokenness. It's a risk because I can't control what they will do with it. I can't harness what everyone else will think or whisper or say about me once they hear my story. I can't keep them from potentially hurting my heart, my spirit, or even my reputation.

But risk is inexorably bound up in faith. As a homebody and a cautious individual, this intertwining between the two is difficult for me; sometimes it feels nearly impossible. I'm not the type who ever wants to skydive or bungee jump or mountain climb. I prefer books and coffee shops and walking tours. *Risk* is not one of my favorite words. But time and again, I find that risk seems to be important to God.

"Faith," I heard a pastor say several years ago, "is spelled R-I-S-K."

Of course, Scripture gets the final word on defining faith, and the book of Hebrews tells us that "faith is the assurance of things hoped for, the conviction of things not seen" (Hebrews 11:1). I understand the connection that pastor was trying to make, though, because being convicted of something we don't see requires a certain amount of risk.

Think of Abraham lifting the knife over his son Isaac. Think of Shadrach, Meshach, and Abednego in the seconds before being flung into the blazing furnace. Think of Daniel praying with his windows open even though he knew a pit of lions was waiting for him. Think of Esther walking down the hallway toward the king without being summoned, knowing her head was on the line. Think of Mary, unwed, saying yes to carrying the Savior. Think of Joseph welcoming a pregnant woman to be his wife when he knew what it would do to his reputation. Think of Matthew, leaving the tax booth and a steady job to follow a poor rabbi. And think of Jesus, hanging on a cross for sins that were not his own, crying out in his anguish for the Father. All these men and women *risked*.[3] They risked their security, their reputations, and their very lives because they believed.

Because they were people of faith.

But risking is scary business. I imagine that Abraham was shaking as he held the knife overhead and that Daniel's knees were knocking when he faced the lions. Mary certainly must have been concerned about what her family—and the town—would think when her belly began to swell. And Jesus himself was so distressed in the garden, knowing the fate that awaited him, that he was sweating drops of blood. Still, these men and women believed in God. They trusted that the rewards of faith far outweighed the risks ahead of them.

One Daring Act

The Bleeding Woman lived out the intertwined reality of faith and risk. We do not really have a modern equivalent of the risk she took by stepping into the crowd that day to reach out to Jesus, but it was immense.

To an outsider, she was just another woman in the crowd, another person passing through. But she knew what her actions might cost her, and she was risking on two levels: as a woman and as an *unclean* woman. One biblical scholar notes that in the first century, women were "expected to display . . . timidity, not daring; and restraint, not boldness."[4] In her decision to chase after Jesus in the jostling movements of a crowd, the Bleeding Woman threw off the timidity and restraint expected of her. She dared to enter the crowd *as a woman*, and her boldness to pursue him was a great risk.

The Bleeding Woman also took a risk by heading into the crowd and aiming for Jesus as an *unclean* woman. There is no way for us to fully immerse ourselves in the cultural milieu of her life; the magnitude of what she was doing in order to get to Jesus was, in essence, grand defiance of the law. With every shoulder she rubbed up against, the Bleeding Woman knew she was making someone unclean. She was rendering every person she bumped into unholy in the sight of the law and therefore unable to enter the Temple. And by touching Jesus, she was making a rabbi—a holy man—unclean before God. Not only that, but she was doing so without his permission! She was well aware that if he found her out or turned on her, she could be judged and humiliated in front of everyone.[5] This woman, who already had no money and no social standing, jeopardized the last thread of her dignity to encounter Jesus.

But it was her only choice. Risk was all that the Bleeding Woman had left.

And if we are honest, risk is all that we have left too.

Risking with God

My waiting hasn't felt very risky. I associate risk with great feats; I see it as something impressive, full of courage and heroism, such as the Bleeding Woman displayed.

But the Lord has started showing me that I *have* taken risks in my journey with trich—not solely because I had to, but because I chose to. God hasn't strong-armed me into risking in this tender area of my life; he has invited me to say yes to risking with him. As I've waited for his healing touch in my life, my risks may not have been visible to those around me, but the Lord knows how much those risks have required of me, over and over and over.

There is the risk of asking him for healing again and again—asking when my heart is weary and vulnerable from continuing to wait.

And there is the risk of trying again—trying to keep my hands down and my mind focused, trying to not pull my eyelashes, even when I feel defeated and worn out.

There is also the risk of hoping again—hoping that I might walk in freedom from this condition someday, even though that hope has been unfulfilled for two decades and often feels like a fool's hope.

No one else sees these risks—they are internal risks that I take with God, choosing to keep my spirit open and vulnerable with him even when he doesn't answer my prayers in the way I wish he would and know he can.

This is the real, hard work of faith for most of us—not jumping off cliffs or swimming in shark-infested waters, but being willing to lay our hearts and souls bare before God without protection or pretense. And it's a risky business.

It's risky to continue to open our hearts to the Lord when our dreams and desires don't line up with reality. Don't let anyone tell you differently. Don't let anyone make you feel like coming to the Lord should always feel warm and fuzzy and easy and clear-cut. It won't. It doesn't.

We are right to tremble. He is God—the Lord of the universe, the Creator of the heavens and the earth, the one who measures the nations as a drop in a bucket (see Isaiah 40:15). And he isn't bound by our ways, our timelines, or our demands. He is bound by truth and love and justice and mercy—by all the things he is and contains within himself.

Why do you think the Bleeding Woman came up behind Jesus? I have no doubt that she was afraid of making him unclean and that she was afraid of risking what shard of reputation she had left by humiliating herself in public. But I imagine that she also had a sense that this Jesus was very powerful. Whether or not she realized he was God, she knew she was approaching someone great and mighty—someone who healed lepers and raised the dead. This was someone who wielded great authority. And so she came trembling. She was right to do so.

When I find myself failing again with trichotillomania, when the pages of my book are dusted with eyelashes and my fingertips are blackened by the mascara I've pulled off, it feels decidedly risky to ask God again to *please heal me*. Because I know that he has heard me for these last twenty years, and cognitively, I know that he is good. But when the answer until now has always been no, and when I choose to come again anyway, I feel exposed before him, and desperate—even like a fool.

I feel emotions I don't like to feel; I come to him as a beggar in need of help. I come to him as a servant to a master, needing the key to a door I can't unlock on my own. I come to him knowing that the answer may be another *no* or *not yet*. And the risk to my heart feels immense, nearly too much to bear at times.

And when it feels like too much to bear, I sometimes come close to giving up. Those are the days when I don't pray about trich, when I try to not think about it, when I give up and give in and just stop trying. Because in risk, there is danger: the danger of having our hearts broken, our bodies shattered, our relationships torn, our welfare stripped away. Any time we risk—with God or with others—life might not go the way we hoped. The person we love may not love us back. The hike up the mountain might end in injury. The hard conversation could end in rejection. The financial investment might flounder. I risk that God will tell me no again and that the healing I want will remain consistently out of my reach. That's the risk we take in being a waiting people—whether we're waiting for what we can hold in our hands or what we desire in our souls.

But we can make the choice to keep risking. In fact, when it comes down to it, risk is the only choice we can really make. "Risk is woven into the fabric of our finite lives,"[6] one theologian writes, because none of us can see into the future. Unlike God, who is all-knowing and all-seeing, we see and know very little of what is ahead. The future always looms cryptically before us like some code we can't yet read, a door with a knob too far from our grasp. Because we can't see what's coming, because we never know how our decisions will ultimately play out, we are risking all the time. We're always banking our hopes on an unforeseen outcome.

The same theologian challenges us with the truth that "there are so many unknowns. . . . Risk is the only way forward."[7] Risk *is* the only way forward, even—and perhaps especially—if it's the continual risking of our hearts before the Lord, the risk of giving him all our desires without knowing what will happen. This is scary business, treacherous heart territory.

But the opposite is even worse. Because if we remain paralyzed and if we refuse to risk staying tender and needy before God, then we are risking something else altogether—something more precious even than the yes we desire from him. If we refuse to risk our hearts with God, then we're missing out on the opportunity for closeness and intimacy with him and with others.

The Gift of Riskiness

Writing this book has forced me to risk telling more people about trichotillomania than I ever have before. Yet there has been a gift in this riskiness, because out of it has come an unexpected freedom.

When friends and acquaintances have asked me about this book, and when I gulped and answered honestly, I was met with a lot of nodding heads. Where I had been expecting looks of confusion, and where I had expected people to change the conversation out of repulsion or awkwardness, I instead found a place where grace cracked wide open. Some people shared their own struggles, the places in their lives where they've been waiting for God to break through for months or years or decades. More than one person told me that they have trichotillomania too—and that they've never talked with anyone else who understands.

Those moments have offered me a surprising gift; I keep finding that as I risk by sharing my brokenness with others, they have shared their brokenness with me. And that intimacy—that shared human communion in places of pain—has been a grace.

Shared brokenness, I have found, does not lead us to despair or to wallowing. Instead, shared brokenness leads us to shared hope. Vulnerability allows me to see my friend for who she is: another soul who is waiting for God to move in her life. In this sacred space, I see another mom who is clinging to the promises of Christ for her child. I see another soul who is holding out faith for God to break through in her story.

If they are all still waiting and holding on and clinging, and if they are hanging on to Jesus in the midst of their own unanswered prayers, then yes, I can continue to do that too. They offer me courage through their stories, and I offer them the same in return. We can hope together. We can trust together. We can experience the gift of God's presence with us and love for us even in the midst of brokenness. And that truly is grace.

What felt so risky to me for two decades—opening up, admitting my weakness, acknowledging the places I've felt shame and struggle and difficulty—has become the soil for beautiful connections with the people in my life.

This place of risk has also become a place of deep connection with God.

Knowing God through Risk

We have to risk if we're going to truly live. And while there is a negative side to risk—the possibility of pain and injury—the truth is that risk also implies possibility. Because without taking risks, few things that matter in our lives will move forward. If we never say we love someone, we might never learn that person loves us in return. If we never hike the mountain, we might never see the sunset glowing with pinks and blues. If we never start the difficult conversation, we might never move into deeper friendship. If we never invest, we might never make more than just enough to survive.

And if we don't risk in our relationship with God—even in the invisible ways of choosing to trust again, hope again, ask again—we might not learn of his goodness and presence in deeper measure. When I open myself to vulnerability with God, I have the opportunity to learn of his kindness and love more richly. These attributes can't be learned any other way. Real love requires vulnerability.

The truth is, to know God requires risking our hearts with him. We know this because we have the best model for risking and living vulnerably before the Father God: Jesus himself. He experienced utmost vulnerability by leaving his throne and becoming one of us, by inhabiting flesh and making himself available to be loved and wounded by his people. And he *was* loved and wounded. His love for us made him vulnerable to us, and ultimately his vulnerability led him to be tortured and killed, and to pay the cost for sins that weren't his own. It wasn't what he wanted; Jesus knew the risk that was ahead of him, and he was filled with sorrow at its coming. He laid his heart bare before the Father, begging for another way—one that wouldn't require the cross and the pain and the suffering:

> Jesus went with them to a place called Gethsemane, and he said to his disciples, "Sit here, while I go over there and pray." And taking with him Peter and the two sons of Zebedee, he began to be sorrowful and troubled. Then he said to them, "My soul is very sorrowful, even to death; remain here, and watch with me." And going a little farther he fell on his face and prayed, saying, "My Father, if it be possible, let this cup pass from me; nevertheless, not as I will, but as you will."

MATTHEW 26:36-39

Jesus prayed this prayer two more times, blood rolling down his cheeks like sweat, pleading with God to spare him the Cross. See that in your mind's eye: Jesus, our strong Savior, pleading with his Father, under duress so great that his blood vessels broke in tiny starbursts across his forehead. The one who tossed the meteors heavenward was on his knees in the dirt, begging for mercy.

Was there ever a greater risk?

In this, Jesus' greatest risk—the risk of his life and his intimacy with his Father—he continued to trust God. Although the answer God ultimately gave was a no—perhaps the hardest no any human has ever heard—Jesus continued to place his hope in his Father. He continued to say yes to God, and in doing so, he defeated death and the grave. And because of his risk, it is his name every knee will bow to, his name every tongue will confess (see Philippians 2:10-11).

Jesus has shown us how necessary risk is. He has shown us that even as we wait for God to move on our behalf, we must be people who risk our hearts with him. Even as we beg God with tears to change our circumstances or to heal our bodies or to reunite a relationship—even then, we must be people who offer him our hearts again.

The Bleeding Woman has shown us the necessity of risk too. She challenges and encourages me; she risked it all. I want the healing she gained, of course, but I also want her faith. I want the boldness and the release of giving everything for an encounter with Jesus.

Because, like her, what else do I have? Jesus is my only hope. No doctor can heal me. No therapy can cure me. Nothing can fix my trichotillomania except a touch from him.

So how do I keep walking in faith in this area of my life where I still need healing? How do I keep saying yes to God in this place in my life where I have no happy ending?

I must, it seems, keep risking. I must keep taking the steps I can toward God, taking a risk on his goodness and his faithfulness and his kindness and his desire to see me whole. And although the risks may not feel huge to anyone else—to those around me, I may just look like another woman in the crowd—to me, they feel immense. But I keep risking in the ways I can by asking him for healing again. I risk by trying to walk in wholeness again, by hoping that I can still be healed. I risk my heart with Jesus because I want to meet him like the Bleeding Woman met him.

I will continue to take the risk of praying for healing. Although I have asked for the Lord to heal me from trich a thousand times over, I will ask again. And I will risk feeling vulnerable before him. Again.

I will continue to take the risk of telling my family and friends that I need prayer and that I need help. I will take the risk of looking weak to them.

I will continue to take the risk of sharing my journey with others and offering them counsel and hope when I can. I will take the risk of seeming odd and broken in order to point others—and myself—back to Jesus.

And through these small things, this faith that I am building, risk upon risk, I'm learning to be sure of what I hope for and certain of what I do not see.

I want to keep choosing faith and the risk that must accompany it. Because the Bleeding Woman met Jesus in her place of risk. And Abraham and Daniel and Mary and Matthew—they all met him there too. It was *when they risked* that they met God most fully in their place of need.

I want to meet Jesus in this place of brokenness. I *need* to meet him here. I know he is good, and I know that he hears me. And that is why I will keep risking my heart with him, in every way I can.

CHAPTER 9

Waiting with Grace

"Who touched me?" The voice carried through the air. To her horror, Sarah saw the rabbi stop. He had been in a hurry, she knew. Why was he stopping?

"Who touched me?" he asked again.

Sarah was up on her feet now, trying to hide at the edges of the crowd. Perhaps if she did not move, the rabbi would not see her. How did he know? It had only been momentary, a mere breath of a touch! Surely he could not have felt that in such a great crowd.

But the rabbi's voice carried over all the others. "Who was it that touched me?" His question was not a demand; Sarah could hear in his voice that he was not angry. The question sounded more like an invitation. "Someone touched me, for I perceive that power has gone out from me."

Sarah's mind whirled. How can I escape? I could run. If I leave quickly, no one will know it was me. *She pulled at her head covering, clenching her fist around the ball of fabric at her neck. Then she fixed her eyes on the ground, ready to run.*

He was walking toward her. "Who touched my garment?" *His voice was steady as a rudder in a calm sea.*

Jesus stopped and stood just a handful of steps ahead of her. Sarah could feel his gaze on her; she kept her face and her tears down. She could not run now. He knows it is me.

Sarah began to tremble. Surely now she would die of shame, *even though she was finally free of her bleeding.*

Kneeling in front of him, Sarah braced herself for ridicule, for the censure she knew she deserved for touching a holy man as an unclean woman.

When he was silent, Sarah looked up.

The eyes that met hers were filled with warmth. There was no anger, no condemnation in his face.

What she found there was kindness.

The tightness in her chest uncoiled. Suddenly Sarah felt safe, at home in her own body and mind. In fact, here in front of Jesus, she no longer felt afraid—not of him, and not of the people pooling behind him like water on a dry riverbed.

On her knees in the dust, Sarah decided she would tell the rabbi everything. For the first time in her life, she did not care what anyone else thought. She cared only what Jesus thought, and she wanted him to know the truth.

Although Sarah knew she should not look a man in the eyes, she also could not take her eyes off him. When she spoke, a voice stronger than she remembered blossomed from her lips. "Rabbi, I have *been bleeding these twelve years. I have seen midwives and doctors; I have offered sacrifices and said hundreds of prayers. I have done everything they have told me to do. But no one has been able to heal me."*

The years were tumbling out of her now, all of them threaded and knotted together in a rush of memory and sorrow. "All the money and gifts that were saved for my dowry I have spent on doctors and cures that never worked. All of my youth I have spent in the darkness of our family home. I have been—" Sarah's voice caught—"I have been so lonely. And I had lost nearly every hope of being healed."

One of the men closest to Jesus started talking. "Rabbi, Jairus's daughter—"

Jesus held up his hand to silence the man and kept his gaze on her. He nodded at her, a soft smile on his lips.

Sarah continued. She could not stop, not now. "After I heard that you could heal even the lepers, I gathered hope that you might be able to heal me, too. But I knew that I would make you . . ." Sarah closed her eyes, struggling to say the word aloud. "I knew, Rabbi, that if I touched you, I would make you unclean." She looked down at the dirt. "I am so sorry, Rabbi."

Jesus still did not move, although the disciples were obviously agitated. At the edges of the crowd, men were grumbling, yelling. But Jesus waited for Sarah to speak.

"When I touched the fringe of your garment, I was healed, right away. I can feel in my body that I am whole again." Tears fell freely down her cheeks and onto the ground. "You have healed me, Rabbi. Thank you."

This is the moment in the Bleeding Woman's life when everything in her story turns on its head: she is healed. Instantaneously, fully, unreservedly—she is made whole.

> She came up behind him and touched the fringe of
> his garment, and immediately her discharge of blood
> ceased. And Jesus said, "Who was it that touched
> me?" When all denied it, Peter said, "Master, the
> crowds surround you and are pressing in on you!"
> But Jesus said, "Someone touched me, for I perceive
> that power has gone out from me." And when the
> woman saw that she was not hidden, she came
> trembling, and falling down before him declared in
> the presence of all the people why she had touched
> him, and how she had been immediately healed.
> LUKE 8:44-47

The Bleeding Woman was given a new chance at life; one touch from Jesus, and she was healed. Yet no matter how many times I read her story, I cannot make it my own. Here, time and again, I hit what seems like a dead end: I am not cured. I want to tell my story differently. But I can't.

I can't wrap up my story nicely. I don't have a way to get around the fact that I'm still struggling with this condition. The narratives I'm used to hearing in church and in books and magazines are the ones that peak at the healing moment, as the Bleeding Woman's does. There is hope and faith, and then there is healing. These are the stories we love to hear—and the ones we hope to be able to tell in our own lives. Not for me. At least, not today. I have hope, yes, and I have faith, but I have not yet experienced healing from trichotillomania. I am still unable to grasp the hem that the Bleeding Woman reached for.

But I can tell you truthfully, with all my heart, that the Bleeding Woman and I are both recipients of grace. It was grace for her to be healed, grace abundant and merciful. And for today, it is grace for me not to be healed.

A Father's Presence

It's not that I don't want to be healed; every day I long to be done with this struggle. But grace is still mine.

When I was four years old, I broke my elbow. It's as bad as it sounds, and I still remember the shock of pain from more than twenty-five years ago—the searing tremor that shot through my arm when the bones cracked and split. It was my first real experience of physical pain, and it lodged itself deep in my memory.

My mother, father, and I had traveled to Michigan to be with our extended family for Christmas. The cousins and aunts and uncles were together in one house, playing and talking and celebrating. Grandpa had a big pool table in the basement, and all of us kids were playing with the pool balls, rolling them over the green felt, making up games that weren't anything like real pool. Somehow I ended up sitting on top of the pool table for one of the games. From there I sent the colorful orbs bouncing from one edge to the other, mesmerized by their movement and the soft thwack of ball against ledge.

The next thing I remember is the pain. I had fallen backwards and sideways, my elbow taking the brunt of the three-foot fall. I wailed; someone ran to get my mom. She carried me to the couch upstairs, and we waited.

We waited because my father was grocery shopping and had taken the only four-wheel-drive vehicle that was available among the nine adults in the house. A snowstorm was raging outside, and my mom knew that trying to get me to the hospital without that car would have been folly. This was years before cell phones, and all we could do was wait for my dad to return.

The pain was so great that I fell in and out of consciousness as my mother stroked my hair. I'm sure my dad wasn't gone for even an hour, but on that couch, the waiting felt like a lifetime. All I knew was that everything hurt. All I knew was that I wanted my daddy to get back so he could help me. I wanted to be with him.

When he came in the front door of the house, covered in snow, my mom told him what had happened. My doctor-father took one look at my arm and piled us into the car without taking his boots off, flipping on the headlights in the dark. I remember little about the drive to the emergency room except that it was dark and snowy. Once we made it past registration, I waited in a white room with my parents.

My mom tried to keep my mind off the pain by asking me about opposites.

What's the opposite of soft? *Hard.*

What's the opposite of hot? *Cold.*

What's the opposite of high? *Low.*

We waited. And we waited some more. We read some of the children's books in the tiny room. We talked about opposites again. I cried. My dad held me. The experience of time is nebulous for children, and I felt like I was suspended in a room of unending waiting. Perhaps I would wait in that little white room, my arm throbbing and hammering, forever.

Finally a doctor came in and ordered an X-ray. My dad was the one who went with me into the X-ray room, and while at the time I didn't understand what was happening, now I know why they let him come in.

In order to determine if my injury was a fracture or a sprain, the technician had to push my arm over my head and flat onto the table. The pain was excruciating; in fact, that pain might have been worse than the pain from my initial fall. My father held my small body still on the table as I cried through the ordeal. He told me he loved me and wasn't going to leave my side.

The X-rays revealed what my father suspected: a fracture in my bone at the elbow. I needed a cast, weeks of rest, and then more weeks of physical therapy.

And that's what I got: a plaster cast heavier than a bowl of rocks, weeks of rest, and more weeks of therapy. I also had to change my fifth birthday party from a bowling party to a hangout party, since I had no use of my dominant arm.

What I also got, thankfully, was a healed elbow. I've never had any complications or issues with that arm after those six weeks in the cast. To this day, my right elbow works just as well as my left, even if it's a bit pointier than its opposite.

I have many memories from breaking my elbow: I remember the pain of that night and the weight of wearing the cast. I remember taking baths with a garbage bag taped over my right arm. I remember the tenderness of my arm unsheathed after weeks under plaster. But what has always stood out to me about the memories from the night I broke my elbow is how much of that experience centered on my father.

My mom was there the whole time, loving and nurturing me, holding me and praying for me. But my memories still point primarily to my dad. I was waiting for him, and I wanted to be with him that entire night. He always knew what to do.

After I fell off the pool table, we waited for him to come back to the house. We waited for him to look at my arm and make a decision, and we waited for him to drive the car through a difficult storm. When there was more suffering ahead, my father was the one who carried me and held me on the X-ray table, and he was the one to comfort me and make sure I wasn't alone with strangers in a dark room. My dad didn't make the pain go away—although I desperately wanted him to—but he was with me *in* the pain. He was the one I waited for, and he was the one who stayed beside me throughout the ordeal. Although he couldn't magically make me better, he made sure I knew that I wasn't alone.

And that, to me, is grace: the grace of a father who never left my side. The grace of a dad who advocated for me and made sure I got the care I needed. The grace of a dad who bought me an ice cream cake for my fifth birthday party when I couldn't go bumper-bowling like I wanted to. He was present with me through all of it.

That is grace.

And that is the grace I've experienced with God in the midst of my struggle with trich. I'm not yet healed, but he has bound me up in a cast of his love. He has been present with me, and he has never left my side. Although at times I have felt alone and angry and frustrated, God is a good Father, and he has been with me through the pain and suffering trich has caused in my life. Through it all, he has told me that he loves me and that he will never leave me.

The grace I have received has not been the grace of healing. It has been the grace of his presence.

A Greater Grace

The Bleeding Woman received the grace of Christ's presence firsthand. She encountered Jesus there in the dirt of a Judean road—and actually, she encountered him twice. She touched him and received the grace of his power filling and healing her body. But she also received the grace of getting to look him in the face and tell him her story. In that moment, she received the grace of his presence again.

When Jesus felt that power leave him, he could have decided to ignore the sensation and head for Jairus's house, knowing that a little girl was dying there. But while a mob of people jostled around him and bumped up against him, he noticed one touch that was different—the touch from the Bleeding Woman. She came to him with the faith that she could be healed, and when she reached out in that confidence, Jesus' healing power was transferred to her.

Jesus knew that someone had come to him in faith. And because of that, Jesus sought her out, not to shame or condemn her, but to offer his presence and his acceptance, to acknowledge her existence and her suffering. There in the dust, he stopped to focus on her and offer her the gift of himself. That was grace to the Bleeding Woman—the presence of Jesus.

My grace has not been the same.

It has been greater.

Although I am not yet healed, the grace I have received is having the presence of Christ with me always. Where the Bleeding Woman waited her entire life—even more than those twelve years—to encounter the living Christ, I daily experience the indwelling presence of Christ within me: the present Holy Spirit.

What grace!

This is the great grace we have been given: we don't have to wait for an encounter with Jesus once in a lifetime or once in a year or even once in a week. For those of us who believe in Jesus and have given our lives to him, we have the indwelling presence of the Holy Spirit every moment of every day. What grace that God would live with us! In our delight and our sorrow, in our joy and our pain, we are never alone. The Bleeding Woman was alone in her waiting for those twelve years. Even when surrounded by people, she was alone on the inside, without a Comforter to meet her in her suffering. She waited without the Holy Spirit.

Our grace is greater! Hear what Christ himself says about the Holy Spirit: "I will ask the Father, and he will give you another Helper, to be with you forever, even the Spirit of truth, whom the world cannot receive, because it neither sees him nor knows him. You know him, for he dwells with you and will be in you" (John 14:16-17).

Although I wait for healing and restoration, I do not wait alone. We have the Spirit of Christ with us always. We are not orphans; we are not fatherless (see John 14:18). God has promised to be with us, now and forever.

That's why I can rejoice, even in my lack of healing. I am with God, even now, although I struggle. He is within me, even when I fail and when I wish my life were different. I am not alone. You are not alone. God is with us.

Jesus has given me more than I ever could have hoped for in giving me himself, and this is a greater grace.

Ultimate Healing

When the Bleeding Woman sought out Jesus, she was seeking healing. All she knew about him, at that point, was that he was a healer. She might have dreamed that he could be the Messiah that Israel was longing for; she might have listened to the rumors that he was more than just a teacher. But the Bleeding Woman had no clear way of knowing that this rabbi was, in fact, the God-man all of creation was holding its breath for and leaning toward. She could not have known, with fullness and clarity, that Jesus was the King of the universe become human for the sake of the world. She met him on the front side of the Cross, and she knew him for what she hoped he was—a healer.

This woman who had been suffering from bleeding and isolation for twelve years assumed that physical healing would be her highest good. She thought physical healing would make her well, in every way imaginable.

What she could not imagine was that Jesus could offer her a recovery better than the physical healing she sought. She could not fathom that there was a healing higher than the stoppage of her bleeding and her constant uncleanness. Her life was one of isolation and sorrow, and she knew that if Jesus could stop her from bleeding, she could also gain her life back.

And that is exactly what happened. With one touch, this woman who had been bleeding and declared unclean by God's law was healed.

This was, by all accounts, a miracle—and for more reasons than one. Yes, her body was healed. But for the first time in twelve years, she was now also clean according to God's law. In biblical times, only uncleanness could be passed from one to another. If someone was unclean—a woman who was bleeding or a person with leprosy, for example—and another person touched them, that person became unclean too (see Leviticus 5:3; 15:25-27). But no one could pass cleanness to someone else. Cleanness came through rituals and proofs—washing with water, offering sacrifices, showing oneself to the priest. In essence, people who were unclean always had to *do* something to gain or prove their cleansing (see Leviticus 14–15).

But there in the middle of a dusty street in a small town in Israel, a miracle occurred twice over. For not only was the

Bleeding Woman healed, but the Rabbi Jesus was not made unclean; in fact, *he transferred his cleanness to her.* No one had ever done this before! No one had ever possessed the power to do such a thing. Any other man would have been made unclean by her touch, but instead, Jesus reversed the order of things, and his touch made *her* clean. And she had not done anything to deserve it. She had not made a sacrifice; she had not performed a ritual; she had not proven she was worthy. As one theologian remarks, "The woman's ritual status did not change him: his status changed her."[1] Miracle!

What a beautiful truth this moment foreshadows: that our status as sinners is changed by the status of Jesus as a perfect, spotless sacrifice. For not long after this encounter, Jesus offered the ultimate cleansing to all who love him and believe in him through his death on the cross and his resurrection from the grave. It was through that great act of love that Jesus transferred his cleanness and his righteousness to us, who are sinful and broken and unclean in the eyes of the law. He took our sin upon himself and gave us his righteousness and purity. He gave us life through his death.

That's why, although the Bleeding Woman experienced great grace in the physical healing of her body, I have experienced a grace even greater.

My body is still broken and my condition still persists, but I have experienced a deeper healing than the Bleeding Woman did that day at the feet of Jesus. You and I live on the far side of the Cross and the Resurrection, and the physical healing I long for—as much as I desire it—is only a shadow of the full healing that will come in the new heaven and the new earth (see Revelation 21:1-4). Even as I wait for that physical healing and that wholeness, the spiritual healing I have received from Jesus is deeper, much deeper, than any other kind of healing.

While the Bleeding Woman got a taste of that grace in her encounter with Jesus, those of us who know him on this side of the Cross have the greater grace: the grace of healing for our souls. Through his death and resurrection, Christ has healed us of the sin that separated us from God. He has transferred his cleanness to us. For while our bodies will one day be healed—either in this life or in the one to come—we already have the grace of spiritual healing that Christ has won for us through the Cross:

> God, being rich in mercy, because of the great love
> with which he loved us, even when we were dead in
> our trespasses, made us alive together with Christ—
> by grace you have been saved—and raised us up
> with him and seated us with him in the heavenly
> places in Christ Jesus, so that in the coming ages
> he might show the immeasurable riches of his grace
> in kindness toward us in Christ Jesus. For by grace
> you have been saved through faith. And this is not
> your own doing; it is the gift of God, not a result
> of works, so that no one may boast.
>
> EPHESIANS 2:4-9

We have been saved! What grace. What amazing, abundant, lavish grace.

For here is the truth: if I were healed physically but didn't have the grace of Christ's presence within me, I would have nothing. If I were freed from trichotillomania but didn't have the grace of salvation and spiritual healing, I would have nothing.

Nothing.

The grace of the Holy Spirit within me and the grace of having my sin washed away so I can have a right relationship with God—these are greater treasures than all the physical healing in the world.

Do I long for healing from trichotillomania? Of course. But even so, I have received immeasurable grace, even without that healing—more grace than I ever could have hoped for.

This is why, on the days when I have to slam my computer shut because I am pulling out too many eyelashes to stay at the library any longer, or on the mornings when I struggle to find any lashes to apply my mascara to, I don't give up hope. Why? Because I am the recipient of extravagant grace.

The Story of Grace

Although the Bleeding Woman received her healing and I have not yet received mine, we are both recipients of enormous grace. And grace has given us both a story to tell.

There, in front of the one who had healed her, the Bleeding Woman poured out her story at his feet. The Scriptures tell us that she "told him the whole truth," that she "declared" her story in the presence of the crowd (Mark 5:33; Luke 8:47).

The Gospel of Luke notes that she fell down in front of Jesus and told her story "in the presence of all the people" (8:47).

She explained "why she had touched him, and how she had been immediately healed." Up until that moment, the Bleeding Woman didn't have a *full* story. She had a sorrow to tell. She had a struggle to relay. But to have a story necessitates a narrative arc with both struggle and resolution. That's the backbone of any powerful tale: a person faces trouble and then experiences resolution.

Until her encounter with Jesus, the Bleeding Woman had only a struggle; she had no solution. Her interaction with Jesus and the sudden stop of her flow of blood gave her a resolution to the pain she had been living in for twelve years. Up until that time, she had only a grief to share. Now she was healed! It was her encounter with Jesus that gave her a story that ended not only in resolution but also in hope.

That hope—that resolution—is what gave her a story to tell. It's why she fell down at his feet and offered her whole story to him. She had been healed, and his presence made sense of the rest of her life.

That's why I have a story to tell too.

Like the Bleeding Woman, I have hope. I have resolution. His grace has given me a story to tell. No, Jesus hasn't given me what I want in this particular part of my life. But although my resolution is not yet complete—I am not healed, and I still wrestle with trichotillomania daily—I have more than I deserve. I have salvation in Christ, and I have his Holy Spirit within me. I have the hope of resurrection and the truth that full healing will come when Jesus returns.

Jesus offers us resolution for our struggle. It may not be immediate and complete resolution in this moment, but it is full and complete resolution for our sin and separation from God.

You have access to this resolution too. Whether you find yourself in a broken marriage or with a troubled mind or in a body that has betrayed you at every turn or with dreams that seem impossible to realize, you still have a story. And if you belong to Jesus, it isn't solely a story of struggle, though it may feel that way.

Lift up your eyes. See the King you are kneeling before, and tell your story with courage. You have a King who has bent to you, who has stopped to listen to you, day after day and year after year. There is hope in his eyes and warmth in his voice. He hears you, he sees you, and he loves you. Jesus may not give you what you want today, and he may not give you what you're asking him for this year or in this lifetime. But he will give you the gift of his presence as you wait, and the gift of salvation and restoration to himself for all eternity.

Those are gifts so big we could spend our whole lives celebrating and still need more wine to pour and more confetti to toss. Those are gifts bigger than any healing, any relationship, any earthly experience or treasure.

No, I am not healed today. I may never be healed this side of heaven. But I am more certain than ever that a day of complete healing is coming. Either it will come soon, or it will finally come on that day when Jesus makes all things new and all things right. And until my day of healing comes, I will tell my story of his presence with me in the midst of waiting.

We won't be in this waiting room forever. We won't

always be staring at the white walls or trying to remember our opposites.

Soon the Great Physician will come, and he will reset every broken bone. He will heal every pain and restore every brokenness. He will renew our strength and wipe away every tear.

He will fulfill all of our longings through his wonderful grace.

He will make us whole.

CHAPTER 10

Hope for the Waiting Ones

Sarah had said all she needed to say. She stayed on her knees, her gratefulness threatening to overtake her. Jesus still had not said anything, but he had not taken his eyes off of her. She would not move until he did.

The crowd waited for the rabbi's response. They were murmuring to one another, unsure whether to heckle her or leave her alone.

Jesus reached for Sarah's hand and raised her to her feet. She stood, unblinking.

"Daughter, your faith has made you well."

Sarah's breath caught in her throat; she felt dizzy with surprise. Daughter? This rabbi has called me *daughter,* one of the people of God?

The voices in the crowd intensified; there was a commotion at the back. Sarah kept her eyes on Jesus.

"Go in peace, and be healed of your disease." He smiled fully and released her hand. She found herself smiling back, perhaps the first true smile she had offered to anyone in a decade.

Healed. She was healed.

Jesus turned to his disciples around him, and they headed in the direction of Jairus's house. Sarah stood, knowing she had been washed in a downpour of love and mercy.

She felt a hand on her shoulder.

Turning, Sarah found herself face-to-face with a mirror, her father. Tears streamed down his cheeks, and he wept openly as he pulled her to his chest. The crowd moved on without them.

Sarah had not known the fullness of her father's embrace for so long, and her tears multiplied as she let herself rest in his arms.

Her father wiped his fist under both eyes and then pulled back enough to cup her chin. "I heard you talking with Rabbi Jesus. And then I heard him speak to you." His eyes were bright as coals from the fire. "Is it true? Are you healed?"

Sarah could not help it; she laughed. "Yes, Abba! He has healed me! I am free." Unbidden, her arms lifted into the air. "Free!"

She had never felt this free in her life. Hope bubbled out of her, wild and honest and full. "And Abba? He called me daughter. Daughter! Does this mean what I hope it means?"

He stroked her hair. "I heard him, Sarah. The whole town heard it. You will come to synagogue now. You are healed, a daughter of Israel. You need never hang your head in shame again."

❦

When I found out I was pregnant, twin emotions rose in me: elation and fear. Elation, because this was a child we had longed and prayed for; we were thrilled that this dream was coming true. But fear bubbled up too; I was scared because suddenly I was carrying life, and we were responsible for another human's existence.

Twenty-one weeks into my pregnancy, we learned that I was carrying a healthy girl—our Ella—and a new set of fears opened to me. I know intimately the struggles of being a woman, and while I worried about the body-image issues and self-confidence struggles she might have, and how she might second-guess her own beauty and purpose, there was one fear that kept floating to the top. With the initial concerns about her health gone, I was now poked and prodded by the fear of passing on trich to her.

Lord, please don't let her struggle with trichotillomania. Don't let this condition become hers, I prayed. Other struggles could be worse, I understood—much worse. But I knew intimately the contours and pains of trich, and I prayed she wouldn't have to know this particular suffering too.

So as I interceded for our little girl while she rolled in my womb, I prayed that she would know Jesus from an early age, that she would be full of peace and health, and that she wouldn't have trich.

The sickness of pregnancy eclipsed many other prayers for me. Hyperemesis, shingles, and sciatica clouded most of my months carrying Ella, and I was never so happy as when I was in labor, knowing that I would meet her soon—and that meeting her would mean the end of being pregnant.

When she was born strong and thriving, I was grateful—more grateful than I knew I could be. I didn't transition easily to motherhood, but my love for her never wavered. She was—and is—one of the greatest joys of my life.

As she passed the one-year mark, I started to worry that she would notice when I stood in front of the mirror checking my lashes or the way I looked at my eyebrows in the rearview mirror at long stoplights, sometimes even pulling them out in the car. I noticed that she watched me while I touched my lash line, and so, with increased resolve, I tried to stop. As she started paralleling my every move, I found new urgency to corral the urge to pull. I didn't want her to mimic me by pulling out her own eyelashes.

I did research, too. I discovered that the children of parents with trich are more likely to develop it, in part because of the genetic tendencies of anxiety and depression that often accompany trich. And although it's not as common, some children develop trich as toddlers, pulling out their hair as a form of self-soothing, similar to thumb sucking or hair twirling.

The conditions could be ripe for Ella. I have trich, she has watched me pull out my own lashes, and her genetic disposition could place her right where I was: achievement-oriented and prone to anxiety. *Oh, Lord, please don't let this condition become hers.* The more fine motor skills she acquired and the more she started replicating my behavior—brushing her hair, using a fork, waving good-bye—the more I started to worry like it was my occupation.

And then one day the fear materialized in front of me. As I was changing her diaper, she reached up with her little fingers and started pulling at her long, beautiful eyelashes. She was a little over two years old.

My heart *thwumped* in my chest, stammering beneath my sternum, white-hot in its urgency. Blood rushed to my cheeks.

"No! *No!*" I yelled, too loudly, too harshly.

Ella looked at me, confused. The start of a cry was on her lips, but she didn't take her hand down.

The guilt of twenty years piled high inside me, and each of my own failures seemed to cascade like a river upon her. Everything in the room felt heavy and slow, as if I were wading upstream in syrup, fighting against the inevitable current.

I inhaled and tried to steady my voice. Covering her hand with mine, I gently drew it down to her side. "No, sweetie. We don't pull out our eyelashes." I knew the hypocrisy even as I spoke it, but I needed to say what I wanted to be true. What I prayed would be true.

I kissed her forehead and tucked my chin down; I didn't want my tears to frighten her or make this moment feel any bigger than it was. I tossed the dirty diaper into the pail and hurried her away as quickly as I could. I wanted her to play in a different room and do something—anything—to keep her hands busy. Coloring, cars, books. Anything else.

I watched her obsessively the rest of the day, trying to swallow the nausea that continued to rise like bile. We ate snacks, we counted crayons, we read stories, we rolled dough and cut shapes. And that night, in the dark, I stared into the muted light behind my eyes.

My worry was coming to life in front of me, and I felt like a charlatan.

If I showed my daughter this action every day of her life, how could I stop her from doing the same? If I pulled out lash after lash, brow after brow, tugging and toying and yanking and grabbing, what else could she know? I—the woman who was shaping womanhood for her—was handing this down like a burden to yoke her neck and her mind.

My very life could lead her to the one thing I didn't want her to have to struggle with.

For weeks I felt sick to my stomach every time I thought about that moment at the changing table. Ella's fingers, still encased in the baby fat she was quickly losing, reaching to pull out the long lashes that framed her blue eyes. Those were the lashes I would have, I knew, if I hadn't ruined mine. But the nausea rose not because I cared about her physical lashes; what I cared about was her heart. Watching her reach to pull out an eyelash represented more than I could name in that moment: decades of fighting against myself, of feeling confused and betrayed by my own body and mind, of hating what I did but being unable to stop.

The guilt was immense, pervasive. I worried about it for weeks, then chastised myself for worrying about it. She was healthy, safe, and loved. In the grand scheme of life, this would be a small thing amid a sea of others, even if she did develop trich. But my love wanted to shield her from the struggle I knew so well.

I knew there were other things I would probably give to her—things I didn't love about myself: my propensity to worry, my love of sugar. But not this, I hoped. *Please, Lord, not this.* Not this thing that seems so small but has worn me down for so long. Not this thing that could so deeply mark her sense of beauty, confidence, and loveliness. So I watched. I waited. I prayed. And I hoped.

Complete Restoration

I have wondered so often about what happened to the Bleeding Woman after her encounter with Jesus. If the years before her moment with the Savior are behind frosted glass, then the years afterward are curtained to us; there is nothing more we can see. When it comes to those twelve years prior to her encounter with Jesus, we at least have some pieces of the puzzle laid before us—a few details, some insights into her life. But Scripture gives us nothing about her life after her healing. She touched Christ's hem, power went out from him, she was healed, and she fell down and told her story.

Then Jesus spoke these precious words to her: "Daughter, your faith has made you well; go in peace, and be healed of your disease" (Mark 5:34).

The writers of the Gospels hasten on from this moment—Jesus was headed to Jairus's house, where he would raise the little girl from the dead. The focus of the scene bounds ahead to that dramatic moment of resurrection. But what was left behind—not just figuratively, but actually—was the formerly Bleeding Woman. Now she was the Healed Woman. What happened to her? Where did she go? What did she do?

All is conjecture from here—imagination dancing on the toes of study. But I love thinking about this, not solely because of what I hope for her but also because of what Jesus spoke to her.

He called her *daughter*. It is not a term that is used loosely—Jesus is intentional in all he says and does. He was speaking identity to her, an identity she had not been able to fully claim for twelve years.

One New Testament scholar and professor writes about this new identity she found after her healing:

> This restoration is not simply a medical healing for the woman. It is a complete restoration. It spells a reversal from a curse that brought with it tremendous social, religious, and, ultimately, personal implications. A woman who lived at the margin of village life is now—before the entire population—restored to a place she has not known for twelve years.[1]

That day Jesus gave the Bleeding Woman a miraculous healing. But more than that, he gave her *restoration*. Through his words and through his kindness and in front of all of her village, Jesus gave this woman her life back. He did not just bandage her up or offer her a temporary fix; he returned her to her original condition; he restored what had been taken away in those twelve agonizing years. Jesus restored her. And her restoration was complete—it included restoration to her community, to God, and even, it seems, to herself.

Restoration to Her Community

In telling her story in front of the crowd, the Bleeding Woman laid her life bare before her village. Her entire future hung on the response of Jesus. They had heard her story; they likely knew of her disease and had avoided her for years. But now she said she was healed. What would the rabbi say?

It was at this critical moment that Jesus affirmed her. Jesus was a rabbi, an authority, a revered man. He had the power to curse her or claim her, and he did the latter by calling her *daughter*. Christ reinstated her as a chosen daughter of Israel and as part of the community.

Previously she had lived on the fringes of God's people. But with one word, Jesus set her squarely in the center of the people of God. She was no longer an outcast but a beloved daughter. She was no longer unclean but acceptable. She could now worship with God's people without fear of reproach or curse.

Restoration to God

Jesus also acknowledged the faith of the Bleeding Woman and noted that it was her faith in him that released her healing: "Your faith has made you well" (Matthew 9:22). While the healing was undoubtedly wonderful, it was not the healing that he praised—it was her faith. Her faith in Jesus' ability was ultimately what restored her to God; her healing was an outward sign of inward faith.

Restoration to Herself

Jesus declared healing over the Bleeding Woman, sending her out in peace. What this woman had longed for so desperately—peace of body, mind, and spirit—was what Jesus restored to her. In the process, he restored her to herself. All the self-loathing, the frustration with her body, the hatred of her circumstances, the emotional distress she endured—it was now gone. She could finally see herself rightly—perhaps for the first time—as a daughter, as a healed one, as one made whole.

All that she had been waiting for was wrapped up in this: peace with God, peace with her people, and peace with herself.

And what did all these things give her? Great joy, I am sure. Probably wonder, perhaps even a bit of holy fear. But I imagine that more than anything else, the restoration Jesus imparted to the Bleeding Woman gave her astonishing hope.

The Glass Wall of Hope

Hope can be a fluttering thing: it is easily fanned into flame and just as easily smothered. But the Bleeding Woman, I am sure, was given great hope the day she encountered Jesus. She had already mustered enough hope to reach out to him in faith, and as the writer of Hebrews explains, it takes hope to have faith at all: "Faith is the assurance of things hoped for, the conviction of things not seen" (Hebrews 11:1). Jesus commended the Bleeding Woman for her faith—she was sure of what she was hoping for, convicted that Jesus could heal her. She had hope enough to reach out to him, faith enough for healing. And then when she was healed, both her faith and her hope must have grown immensely, because Jesus was who she had hoped he was, and even more besides. He restored not only her body but also her soul and her life.

Her hope must have been boundless! She had been waiting for this moment for twelve years, not knowing if it would ever come. Now where there had only been sorrow and darkness, Jesus had given the Bleeding Woman hope. Her hope for the future must have been untold and unrestrained. It must have been wild!

That is what restoration does. It brings hope—hope that the future can and will be better than what we have known. Hope that what is ahead is better than what is behind. Hope that can stand in the midst of trial, in the midst of pain, in the midst of struggle.

There is one truth that allows us to be a people of hope, even as we wait for our own wholeness and healing: Jesus has restored us to himself, to others, and to ourselves. And when the King of kings restores us—soul, body, and life—we are given hope, not only for this life, but for all of eternity.

Our restoration to God is already complete; Christ accomplished that through his death and resurrection. He has paid the price for our sins and restored us to a right relationship with God (see Romans 5:11). We have hope in the coming Kingdom and hope in the coming return of our King.

But our restoration to others and to ourselves is still unfolding. It's not yet finished.

This is where things get muddy. This is where our hope is most often battered, where it is so easily smothered, as we await that full restoration. For our bodies still betray us and our minds still quake with fears and anxieties. Our relationships with our family members and friends still strain and sometimes fracture. Our desires and our dreams so often dissolve before us. Life is hard. Our hearts grow weary. Hoping feels too tender, too raw. Waiting for the fullness of our promised restoration threatens to usurp our hope.

I've been here so many times with trich, where the hoping has felt too risky, too vulnerable. Hope feels like a foul trick our hearts play on us, wheedling us on with dreams that never crystallize. The healing doesn't come, the job doesn't materialize, the relationship doesn't last.

Waiting is hard because it thwacks against our hope and makes us wonder if the promises of Christ are real. It makes us wonder if Jesus is really good.

Waiting often pushes our buttons. It pushes our buttons of anxiety and shame. It pushes our buttons of weakness and worry. It pushes our buttons of identity and worth. In all of those places, waiting asks us if God is still good and if he really sees and loves us.

Hope is the glass wall covering those buttons, providing protection for our hearts while we wait. Although it may get walloped and slammed against, hope is the antidote to despair, and it's the only way to live through prolonged seasons of waiting without losing our faith or our sanity.

Because hope—when it's founded in Christ—will never truly disappoint us. If our hope is in a person or a job or an opportunity or our own bodies, then it will vanish like a mirage in the dust. Hope in anything other than Christ will fail.

But hope in Jesus and in his coming Kingdom—and the complete restoration to our Lord, ourselves, and the community that will exist there—never disappoints. Paul writes about this in his letter to the Romans. Paul—who knew greater suffering and trials than most of us could imagine but who never lost his hope in Christ—says something about restoration that is just as applicable today as when he first penned the words.

> Since we have been justified by faith, we have peace with God through our Lord Jesus Christ. Through him we have also obtained access by faith into this grace in which we stand, and we rejoice in hope of the glory of God. Not only that, but we rejoice in our sufferings, knowing that suffering produces endurance, and endurance produces character, and character produces hope, and hope does not put us to shame, because God's love has been poured into our hearts through the Holy Spirit who has been given to us.
>
> ROMANS 5:1-5

According to Paul, our faith has placed us under grace, and in that place we rejoice in our hope of the glory of God. In fact, our hope is so great that we can rejoice even in our suffering, knowing that these struggles—trich, disappointment, disease, sickness, pain, sorrow, death, delay—are developing goodness in us. As we suffer and wait for the fullness of God's Kingdom to be revealed, he develops endurance, character, and hope in our hearts. And hope does not put us to shame.

We, the waiting ones, will not be put to shame as long as our hope is in Jesus. That hope is not a false hope. In fact, it's the truest hope of all; it's the hope that is even now coming true.

That's why I still have hope with trichotillomania, why I still ask God to heal me, and why I still allow a flame to flicker in my heart that I will be healed. I have hope because my hope is not in being healed from trich. My hope is in the Savior who loves me and has saved me.

I know that as I continue to walk through this struggle, God is developing goodness in me, and this goodness is leading me to even more hope in him. But I can't let my hope be swayed by what I see with my eyes. As Paul writes to the church in Corinth, "If in Christ we have hope in this life only, we are of all people most to be pitied" (1 Corinthians 15:19).

If I heaped my hope only on what I saw at the end of each day—my bare lash line, the eyelashes covering my keyboard, the bald patches in my eyebrows—I would be hopeless in this area of my life. But I'm choosing to put my hope in Jesus rather than in my circumstances. I continue to put my hope in his goodness and in his ability and in his grace rather than in my own strength or willpower. And that's why my hope can't be shaken—in trich or in any struggle—because my hope doesn't depend on me. It doesn't depend on the outcome of my situation. It depends on Jesus and on his power.

But does that mean we can't hope for healing and wholeness now? Not at all. We have hope for both today *and* eternity—but we can't confuse the one for the other. We can't confuse our hope for today with the only hope we have. So our hope is for the here and now, and we believe that God is the God who still heals and saves and delivers in our present, *here*, in what we can taste and touch and see and smell. But that's not where our hope finds its end. We must aim our hope not solely in this life but also in the coming life.

This is the now and the not yet of life in Christ: we are restored, and we are being restored, and we will finally be fully restored when Christ returns and makes all things new (see Revelation 21:1-7). Though we suffer many trials and tribulations now, our hope is tucked in the truth of the gospel of Jesus Christ—and this is a hope that won't put us to shame.

So I hope unreservedly in Christ for my healing. I don't demand that he heal me now, though I ask him to. But I hope—and I have faith—that God will heal me fully, whether in this life or in the one to come.

Interrupted by Love

I continued to worry about my daughter developing trich. In my mind, I kept replaying that moment when she reached for her eyelashes and tried to pull them out. I prayed, I begged, I tried not to think about it. And I watched her carefully for weeks.

I asked God over and over to help her, to help me, to stop this for both of us. For the first time I wanted to be free not just for myself but also for my daughter. I wanted freedom so that she could have it too.

But as weeks and then months went by and she didn't

reach for her lashes again, my worry started to abate and then dissolve. I've never seen my daughter pull on her eyelashes again. Still, in quiet moments, worry pops up, the fear rising like helium and threatening to carry me away.

One day while I was praying, God interrupted my fears with a question:

Would your love for your daughter alter if she had trich?

"Of course not," I whispered.

Would your affection for her lessen?

"Never."

Would the calling I have on her life change?

I knew it wouldn't. "No, Lord."

Where is your hope? Is it in me, or is it in what happens to her?

I paused. "It's in you, Lord. Solely in you."

Then have no fear, daughter. There is no fear in my love.

And in that moment, in that revelation, I understood afresh how God saw me.

Has his love for me ever altered as I've fought with trichotillomania or as I've waded through a thousand other struggles, sins, and pains?

Of course not.

Has his affection for me lessened or wavered in the years I've had trich or when I've been disgusted with myself?

Never.

Has the calling on my life ever changed because of this weakness, this struggle?

No.

Has my hope ever been dependent upon what I can see, or is it dependent upon whom I will follow?

It is dependent upon Christ alone.

Then I will have no fear, being a woman who walks in his love.

And we will have no fear, being those who walk in his love. For we are the restored ones. We are the waiting ones. We are those who are both restored already and yet are still waiting—waiting for the fullness of his restoration and his Kingdom. But we wait with great hope and great joy. We are the ones with our eyes always tilted upward, always holding our breath in the hope that today will be the day the King returns. And we are the ones who are learning there's nothing to fear, because nothing can keep us from his love. No struggle, no trial, and no suffering can keep his unquenchable love from us (see Romans 8:35-39).

The Bleeding Woman was restored and made whole. And while I still have trichotillomania, I have been restored and made whole in Christ. I have not yet experienced the fullness of that restoration, but it will come.

Your restoration is here. And your full restoration will come too. In Christ, I promise you, it will come.

For now, we wait. But we have hope in our waiting, whatever it is we are waiting for: hope that Christ is with us, hope that Christ is for us, hope that Christ is coming again.

Hope that one day, like the Bleeding Woman, we will be made whole when we encounter Jesus face to face.

May that day come quickly. May we meet him soon.

Come, Lord Jesus!

The Unexpected
Sweetness of Waiting

*S*arah's father put his arm around her shoulders, and they stood, side by side, facing the road that led home. "Let us go and tell your mother," he said. "She will be so happy, Sarah—happier than we have seen her in a long, long time." He was looking toward their family house, his feet already set in that direction.

"I want her to know, Father. She has prayed for me these twelve years." Sarah turned in the direction Jesus and his disciples had gone. Her heart pointed a clear arrow. "But I must go and follow Rabbi Jesus. He has healed me. He has given me hope! I want nothing more than to be where he is."

A flicker of uncertainty crossed her father's face, and he breathed deeply. Sarah waited for him to speak.

When her father looked up again, his eyes were clear. He

nodded slowly, then kissed her forehead. "Go, Sarah. Do what you must. There will always be a place for you in our home."

Sarah bowed before him and squeezed his hand.

And then she turned to Jairus's house.

She would follow Jesus, no matter where he went.

I recently planted a tiny garden in front of our home. To anyone who knows me, this fact is probably startling, not to mention laughable. I've never gardened in my life, and I've even succeeded in killing the succulents I was gifted—plants that are supposed to be impervious to horrible care. I have friends who love being in the dirt and planting their gardens, who love watching the leaves uncoil and the blossoms unfurl. They adore the cycle of life they see there, and they take joy in participating in the mysterious process that plants and flowers display.

My next-door neighbor Amber is one of those people. She has only a small, uneven plot of gardening space, but in it she grows a veritable greenhouse of tomatoes and thyme and beans and melons. She cares for a blossoming rosebush and checks her basil every day. Amber loves her garden and tends to it carefully, and she is teaching her daughter to do the same.

About a month ago, when everything in her yard was starting to blossom, I looked at the dying grass in front of our house and realized that our little plot of land, sandwiched between two neighbors with beautiful gardens, looked sloppy. Careless, even. We all live in seminary housing, and the school offers us fifty dollars every spring to "beautify" the area in front of our homes for the common good. It seemed I wasn't doing my part.

In that moment, I made a split-second decision to start a garden. I told Ella that we were leaving to buy some flowers for the yard. "Perennials, so I'll never have to try this again," I whispered to her under my breath.

It ended up taking us two trips to the store. The first time I came back with flowers but no gardening spade, and pavers but no mulch. As comfortable as I am around words and people, I am clumsy and confused around dirt and growing things. I love looking at plants, but I have no idea how to help them thrive.

So after talking to Amber and learning that I would definitely need a spade and mulch and something called "weed barrier fabric" to prep the flower bed, I scooted Ella back into the car and asked for help at the nursery. We returned home with the needed items, plus a cantaloupe plant that came in a biodegradable cup. Ella loves cantaloupe, and when I saw it on the shelf, I asked her if she wanted to try to grow it together. Did I have any experience growing fruit? No. But how hard could it be to grow a plant that comes in its own cup?

"Cantaloupe? Yes! I love cantaloupe!" She giggled and held the cup in her hands all the way to the checkout lane.

The flowers sat in their plastic pots on our window ledge for four or five days; the pavers were stacked in two piles by our front door. I stared them down every time I walked into the house, but I didn't know how to start. I was insecure. I felt silly for even thinking about growing a garden. And then Ella asked me about the cantaloupe. She wondered when it would grow and when those tiny leaves poking out of the cup would turn into the fruit she wanted to eat. Looking at her face, I realized that if I didn't at least *try* to plant the flowers and our cantaloupe plant, they would die on the ledge, and I'd have to explain to her that I'd killed the cantaloupe. Plus, we would be out fifty bucks.

I wasn't wearing the right shoes, and my spade was too small, but I decided to plant a garden that day. I cleared the ground, laid down the weed barrier fabric, and dug some holes. It wasn't pretty, and I don't like getting dirt under my fingernails, but I kept at it, sweat rolling down my neck. The flowers went into the ground, and I edged our little garden with stone pavers that ended up looking like they were laid by a careless mason.

But I did it. I planted a garden.

When I stood up to survey my work, I realized that I hadn't yet planted the cantaloupe. It was still sitting on the ledge. But there was space in the back corner for the plant, and after digging one final hole, I nestled the cup into the earth.

"Ella, this is our little garden!"

"Where's the cantaloupe?" She asked. She knew what she wanted.

"Do you see those little green leaves right there?" I pointed to the tiny cantaloupe shoots, newly placed in the ground.

"Yes! When will it grow?"

I looked at the label. Ugh. Mature fruit takes close to

seventy-five days. Maybe I'd chosen the wrong plant for a toddler.

I pushed the hair and sweat off my face. "Well, sweetie, it's going to take a *very* long time for this cantaloupe to grow. Past your birthday, and even longer after that."

"Longer than my birthday?"

I nodded. We had been talking about her birthday for months, and there were still several weeks before her party. In her life, her birthday was the most far-off thing she could imagine. And yet she seemed unfazed by the timeline I'd described. After we watered the flowers together, I tossed the spade in the grass and went inside to wash my hands.

Childlike Hope

Several weeks after we planted the cantaloupe, the time came for Ella's third birthday party, complete with princess dresses and a chocolate cake. She had a wonderful time; I nearly cried when we sang "Happy Birthday" to her and the room swelled with the voices of people who love her—and us—so well.

As we sat down to eat dinner that night, we started talking about the day and the party.

Ella piped up, "The cantaloupe Mommy and I planted will take a long, long time to grow." She paused. "But after I turn four, it will be ready!" She threw her hands up in the air.

I looked at her, startled by her comment. We hadn't mentioned the cantaloupe plant for days, maybe a week. And we'd never talked about her having to wait until she turned four. But she understood, at least on some level, that turning four wasn't going to happen for a long time.

I looked at her eyes, bright with anticipation, and realized that she had such hope! Ella trusted that this little cantaloupe plant would grow into the fruit she loved, even if it took a very, very long time, and even if her mother was a reluctant and mediocre gardener at best.

I squeezed her arm. "That's right, sweetie. That cantaloupe is going to grow, and it will be here even *before* your fourth birthday."

She squealed. "Yay!"

Savoring the Sweetness

Ella's hope surprised me—both on her birthday and now, as we continue to wait for the plant to blossom. She wants this cantaloupe dearly, although she doesn't know how or when it will grow. But she believes that it will, and she trusts that it will, and she is willing to wait for it to come to fruition even though time is hazy and vague to her. She's even willing to wait a quarter of her life—until she's four!—for this plant to grow, all the while trusting that she will one day savor the sweetness of her waiting.

Her childlike faith is teaching me so much about hope. Because I know what I'm wanting and waiting for too.

I want healing, although I don't know how or when it will happen. But I believe that it will, and I trust that it will, and I'm willing to wait for it to come to fruition even though the timeline is hazy and vague to me. And thankfully, my hope is even surer than hers. Unlike a cantaloupe plant in the hands of an unskilled gardener, my life is in the hands of a faithful and loving God, the one who is never reluctant to help me or give me what I need. I can live in the hope that God will grow me into who I'm meant to be and that he will ultimately heal me, even if it doesn't take place for a very, very long time. I've already waited a quarter of a lifetime, and even if I have to wait the whole of an earthly lifetime, I know that one day I will savor the sweetness of my waiting.

In the meantime, I can trust that I'm in the loving hands of the most skilled gardener of the body and the soul. He waters and grows and cares for us perfectly and lovingly, knowing exactly what we need to thrive and develop into who he has made us to be. Our waiting is understood and tended to by him—the kindest and best gardener of all, the King who will one day make everything blossom in stunning color and in perfect timing.

Ella is waiting for those leaves in the back of our garden to turn into a round, juicy fruit. I am waiting for the restoration of my body and mind from trichotillomania. Really, both of us are waiting for wholeness. And as I wait for the buds of the new heaven and the new earth to break through the soil of this current earthly reality—as I wait for Christ to usher in his coming Kingdom with fullness—I, like Ella, will wait with hope.

I am hoping expectantly for the coming Kingdom, knowing that if I walk with Christ forever on this earth with trichotillomania but still get to be by his side, that is enough for me. I am hoping in his love and comfort, trusting that if he's with me in the midst of my sorrow and struggle, he will be sufficient for me. I am hoping in his goodness and his truth, understanding that if I continually find myself walking in weakness but he is my portion, I will be satisfied. He is good, and he is my healer. Today or tomorrow or at the end of all days—one day I *will* be healed. One day the bud will burst forth into blooming. Until that day, I will stay as close to Jesus as I can, following where he leads. Because I know that on that day, I will no longer be like the Bleeding Woman, grasping for his hem.

I will be in his arms.

ACKNOWLEDGMENTS

The opportunity to write this book has been nothing but grace at every stage, and there are many people who have played a part in bringing this book to life. My deepest thanks go to these wonderful men and women:

To Kara Leonino, who championed this book from the start—thank you for taking a risk on me and for giving me the grace of a chance. You have been not only an incredible editor but also a trusted friend.

To Stephanie Rische, who strengthened not only my words but my spirit—it has been an honor to partner with you in shaping this book and to be the recipient of your expertise and your encouragement.

To Jon Farrar, who offered this book a home, as well as insight and wisdom along the way—thank you!

To the entire team at Tyndale—you are a dream come true. Working with you has felt like joining a family I didn't know I had. Thank you for partnering with me and for believing in me.

To Jess Connolly, who wrote the foreword for this

book—you are a sister who is running straight toward Jesus, and I'm grateful for your friendship.

To those who taught and encouraged me in this love of writing—I am indebted to you. Jeff Davis, you modeled how words could draw the soul to God, and it set my heart aflame. David Wright, you led me toward deeper creativity in my words with levity and intention. Wayne Martindale, your tenderness toward Christ in your teaching shaped my love of God and my writing. Lauren Winner, this book was born under your guidance, under your expert eyes and kindness. As teachers, you have all shaped me deeply. Thank you for doing the meaningful and eternal work of training up the generations after you.

To Nita Martindale—thank you for mentoring me and pointing me to the Lord at every turn. Your heart is gold.

To the board and the members of the Redbud Writers Guild, who have cheered for me and helped me—your sisterhood is a gift. The Wheaton manuscript group shaped this text in its initial stages, and I am so thankful!

To Mike and Sara Baker, who have led and loved their church for so many years and who have helped me to love Jesus since I was in junior high—thank you. Michael and I are grateful for your leadership and friendship in our lives. You are worthy of great honor in the Kingdom of God.

To Jess, Jen, Kayla, Emily, and Mary—your friendships are invaluable to me. Thank you for your consistent love and kindness, even in the midst of my own brokenness and struggle. Yours are some of the sweetest friendships I have known. I love you!

To Elsie—thank you for extending grace to me for so many years of our friendship. I hold you dear.

To Gwen, Christie, Katie, Gabrianne, Andrea, Meagan, Kerilee, and Constance—so much of this book was written as we walked together. Thank you for helping me experience his grace in this journey. I'm so thankful for your love for Jesus and for how you have helped me love him more!

To Kristi, Ashley, and Shelly—it is a blessing to spur one another on as writers and as Christ followers. Thanks for sharpening my heart and my pen.

To the Hoxie family—thank you for loving our family so dearly. Robyn, you walked this road with me for so many years, always with grace and tenderness. We are cheering you on!

To Rebekah and Dillon—you have been dear friends who are conduits of God's love and kindness to us. We praise the Lord for your lives and leadership.

To my Writing with Grace students, who have believed in and with me—thank you for your trust and your tenacity in following your calling as writers. Your obedience to the Lord heartens me!

To Cathy and Jim, my in-laws—I am so grateful for your love, support, and encouragement. You have cheered me on constantly, and I'm blessed to be a part of the Swindell family.

To Steven, Fallon, Christine, and Manly—you have given me nothing but love in all our years of being family. I love calling you my siblings!

To my sister, Claire—yours has been the deepest and most treasured friendship I have ever had. Thank you for walking with me in the midst of trial and celebration, and for loving me unreservedly. And to Wade—thank you for loving me as a sister and for loving our family like Jesus does.

To my parents—where to start? It is your love that buoyed and strengthened me countless times over this particular journey and the many others I have walked through. You pointed me to Jesus and demonstrated his love and kindness in our family unwaveringly. You still do. Thank you for loving and leading me. I am eternally, eternally grateful for you.

To Ella—you are the sweetest treasure God has given to us. You are a bright and shining light, a joy and a gift. I love being your mom, and I love who you are—and who you are becoming. I will always be here for you, no matter what the future holds.

To Michael, my dearest love—thank you for being the biggest encouragement in my calling as a writer; thank you for the practical and prayerful ways you have enabled me to see this book to completion. In your gaze, I have felt the love of God most surely. Thank you for being a man devoted to Jesus and devoted to me. Thank you for loving me and Ella wholeheartedly. You help me love the Lord more; you have extended more grace to me than can be measured. I feel privileged every day to be your bride.

To the triune God: Father, Son, and Holy Spirit—you have saved, restored, and renewed me; my heart is yours! All that I am and have belongs to you. Thank you for giving me life; may you be glorified in it, in every way.

NOTES

CHAPTER 1: WHEN WAITING MAKES YOU BROKEN

1. "Trichotillomania Statistics: The Numbers behind Hair Pulling Disorder," *TrichStop*, accessed November 7, 1016, http://www.trichstop.com/info /general/trich-statistics.
2. Samuel R. Chamberlain, Lara Menzies, Barbara J. Sahakian, and Naomi A. Fineberg, "Lifting the Veil on Trichotillomania," *The American Journal of Psychiatry* 164, no. 4 (April 2007): 568–74, http://ajp.psychiatryonline.org /doi/full/10.1176/ajp.2007.164.4.568.

CHAPTER 2: WHEN WAITING MAKES YOU WEAK

1. C. S. Lewis, *The Weight of Glory* (New York: HarperOne, 2001), 37.
2. Harvey Simon, ed., "Anemia," *University of Maryland Medical Center*, last reviewed March 18, 2013, http://umm.edu/health/medical/reports/articles /anemia.
3. Michelle Wright and Colin Tidy, "Iron-Deficient Anaemia," *Patient.info*, last reviewed November 24, 2014, http://www.patient.co.uk/doctor/iron -deficiency-anaemia-pro.
4. "Lexicon: Strong's G769: Astheneia," *Blue Letter Bible*, https://www .blueletterbible.org/lang/lexicon/lexicon.cfm?Strongs=G769&t=ESV.
5. Ibid.

CHAPTER 3: WHEN WAITING COSTS YOU EVERYTHING

1. See David Instone-Brewer, "Choosing a Legal System in Early Judaism," http://www.tyndale.cam.ac.uk/Tyndale/staff/Instone-Brewer/LegalSystems .htm, for more information regarding dowries in Jewish culture. Article forthcoming in *Review of Rabbinic Judaism: Ancient, Medieval, and Modern*, http://booksandjournals.brillonline.com.

CHAPTER 4: WHEN WAITING CLAIMS YOUR IDENTITY
1. R. C. H. Lenski, *The Interpretation of St. Mark's Gospel* (Minneapolis: Augsburg Fortress, 2008), 220–21.
2. Darrell L. Bock, *Luke*, The IVP New Testament Commentary Series (Downers Grove, IL: InterVarsity Press, 1994), 159.
3. Ibid.
4. William L. Lane, *The Gospel of Mark*, 2nd ed., The New International Commentary on the New Testament (Grand Rapids, MI: Eerdmans, 1974), 191.
5. Bock, *Luke*, 159.
6. C. S. Lewis, *The Weight of Glory* (New York: HarperOne, 2001), 42.

CHAPTER 5: WHEN WAITING FEELS OFFENSIVE
1. Elisabeth Elliot, *Passion and Purity* (Grand Rapids, MI: Revell, 2002), 89.
2. Elisabeth Elliot, *Quest for Love* (Grand Rapids, MI: Revell, 2002), 133–34.
3. James R. Edwards, *The Gospel according to Mark*, The Pillar New Testament Commentary (Grand Rapids, MI: Eerdmans, 2002), 163.
4. Ibid.

CHAPTER 6: WHEN WAITING BRINGS YOU SHAME
1. Steven Phillipson and Christopher Gibson, "Hair Pulling a.k.a., Trichotillomania: A Simple Habit or a Complex Diagnosis?" Center for Cognitive-Behavioral Psychotherapy, *OCD Online*, accessed September 9, 2016, http://www.ocdonline.com/trichotilomania.
2. James R. Edwards, *The Gospel according to Mark*, The Pillar New Testament Commentary (Grand Rapids, MI: Eerdmans, 2002), 163.
3. Samuel R. Chamberlain, Lara Menzies, Barbara J. Sahakian, and Naomi A. Fineberg, "Lifting the Veil on Trichotillomania," *The American Journal of Psychiatry* 164, no. 4 (April 2007): 568–74, http://ajp.psychiatryonline.org/doi/full/10.1176/ajp.2007.164.4.568.

CHAPTER 7: WHEN WAITING FEELS LIKE SUFFERING
1. Hugh Grubb, "Recovering from the Trauma of Trichotillomania," *Trichotillomania Learning Center Newsletter*, 1997.
2. "About Masiphumelele," *Masicorp*, accessed November 4, 2016, http://www.masicorp.org/aboutmasiphumelele.html. See also "Masiphumelele," *Living Hope*, accessed November 4, 2016, http://www.livinghope.co.za/about/communities/masiphumelele.

CHAPTER 8: WHEN WAITING IS RISKY
1. Gary M. Burge, *Encounters with Jesus* (Grand Rapids, MI: Zondervan, 2010), 6.

2. Ibid., 47.

3. See Genesis 22; Daniel 3; 6; Esther 4–5; Luke 1; Matthew 1; 9; 27.

4. Bruce J. Malina and Jerome H. Neyrey, "Honor and Shame in Luke-Acts: Pivotol Values of the Mediterranean World," in *The Social World of Luke-Acts: Models for Interpretation*, ed. Jerome H. Neyrey (Peabody, MA: Hendrickson, 1991), 42.

5. Burge, *Encounters*, 48.

6. John Piper, *Risk Is Right: Better to Lose Your Life Than to Waste It* (Wheaton, IL: Crossway, 2013), 19.

7. Ibid., 20.

CHAPTER 9: WAITING WITH GRACE

1. Gary M. Burge, *Encounters with Jesus* (Grand Rapids, MI: Zondervan, 2010), 53.

CHAPTER 10: HOPE FOR THE WAITING ONES

1. Gary M. Burge, *Encounters with Jesus* (Grand Rapids, MI: Zondervan, 2010), 48.

DISCUSSION QUESTIONS

Chapter 1: When Waiting Makes You Broken

1. The Bleeding Woman experienced a major—and unwanted—change in her life when she started bleeding. Have you experienced any changes in your life (large or small) that were unwanted or difficult? How have those changes affected the course of your life?

2. Ann's struggle with trichotillomania forced her to start coming to terms with her own brokenness because she couldn't do anything to fix it. What are you waiting for God to heal, fix, or renew in your life?

3. Are there any good sides to brokenness? How might the brokenness you feel be a gateway to knowing God's love in a new way?

4. Moving forward: Spend some time in prayer, asking God to show you his love through your brokenness.

Chapter 2: When Waiting Makes You Weak

1. Ann shares that, with trich, she often felt that she should "try harder" and be able to "get it together." Have you ever felt weak in the one area you wanted to be strong? What happened?
2. The Bible says that God's power is made perfect in our weakness (see 2 Corinthians 12:9). What do you think this verse means?
3. Ann writes, "The ways I fail and the ways I don't measure up actually act as a vehicle to meeting Jesus in my daily life" (page 42). In what ways have you seen God work in the weak areas of your life or the lives of those you love?
4. Moving forward: Write down the places in your life that feel weak, and ask Jesus to show you how those places provide an opportunity to meet with him in a deeper way. Take note of how he meets you in the coming days.

Chapter 3: When Waiting Costs You Everything

1. The Bleeding Woman spent all her money seeking healing. Have you ever spent a lot of money, time, or energy trying to fix an area of brokenness in your life? Did it work?
2. Ann shares that hiding trichotillomania from her friends cost her a great deal in terms of time, energy, and friendship. Have you ever tried to hide a weakness from those closest to you? What did it cost you?

3. We can rest in knowing that Jesus has already paid the highest price for our struggles through his death on the cross (see 1 Peter 1:18-21). What would it look like to admit our inability to be self-sufficient (see page 60) and invite the Lord into our weakness and waiting? How might our lives—and our friendships—be transformed?

4. Moving forward: Read 2 Corinthians 3:4-5 out loud, and then thank the Lord that "our sufficiency is from God," not from ourselves. Pray for the grace to rely on him this week.

Chapter 4: When Waiting Claims Your Identity

1. Ann writes about how she always wanted to be identified as "beautiful." How do you long to be identified?

2. One of the reasons Ann struggled with her weakness was because "it slithered into [her] identity" (page 69). Are there any areas in your life where you identify yourself by your struggle, your sin, or what you lack?

3. In Christ we have a new identity that is determined not by our brokenness or sinfulness but by his love. What practical steps can you take this week to focus your heart and mind on how Christ identifies you?

4. Moving forward: Write out one or two verses that declare your identity in Christ (Ephesians 2:10 and 1 Peter 2:9 are great places to start). Read them every day, reminding yourself of who you truly are.

Chapter 5: When Waiting Feels Offensive

1. When God says no to what we want, it's easy to take offense. Are there any places in your life where you are feeling offended by God? What prompted those feelings?
2. The Bleeding Woman kept her heart tender toward God because she clung to hope. In what area of your life do you need more hope in God's love for you?
3. What's the difference between being honest with God and being offended by him? What can you do to remain tethered to God when you're on the brink of offense?
4. Moving forward: Make a list of times in your life when you have felt offense toward God, and ask him to forgive you. Tear the paper into pieces and throw the pieces away. Then read Romans 8:28, and ask the Lord to increase your trust in his love for you.

Chapter 6: When Waiting Brings You Shame

1. Ann has struggled with shame over trichotillomania for most of her life. Has the feeling of shame ever played a role in your life? How?
2. The lie of shame is that it pairs our worth with our weakness. In what ways have you believed the lie that your worth is directly connected to your weakness, sin, or struggle?
3. Hebrews 12:2 says, "For the joy set before him [Jesus] endured the cross, scorning its shame, and sat down at the right hand of the throne of God" (NIV).

What do you think it means that Jesus scorned the shame of the cross? What might it look like to scorn the shame in your own life?

4. Moving forward: Take some time this week to reject the power of shame in your life by accepting the freedom Christ has won for you. Read Romans 8:1; Romans 5:6-11; and 1 John 3:19-20, and thank the Lord for what he has done.

Chapter 7: When Waiting Feels Like Suffering

1. Ann says that the Bleeding Woman's suffering was significant to Jesus. "He understood that her waiting had been part of her suffering—that the waiting itself had *caused* her suffering" (page 155). Have you ever felt like your pain wasn't as significant as someone else's pain? How do you think Jesus would view your suffering?

2. Ann writes, "I didn't have to worship my pain with hymns and praise to let it be the driving force in my life. I just had to let it uproot God as the central focus" (page 160). Has suffering ever become the driving force in your life? What was the result?

3. Ann writes, "Jesus can affirm our suffering because *he has suffered it with us*" (page 161). How does your perspective on your suffering change when you realize that Jesus suffered too?

4. Moving forward: Take some time to pray this week, asking Jesus to reveal his nearness to you in your suffering and to give you new perspective on how he

has suffered with you. Read John 19, and thank Jesus for what he has already suffered on your behalf on the cross.

Chapter 8: When Waiting Is Risky

1. The Bleeding Woman took a risk by reaching out as an unclean woman to touch Jesus. Have you ever taken a big risk with something close to your heart? What happened?

2. It feels risky to continue to open our hearts to the Lord when our dreams and desires don't line up with reality, but it would be far worse to miss the opportunity to grow in closeness and intimacy with God. In what ways are you holding back your heart from the Lord? What risk is he calling you to take?

3. It's a risk to tell others about our brokenness, because we can't control how they will respond. But opening up to others actually paves the way for deep connection. Is there someone you need to risk being vulnerable with—someone who needs to hear your heart?

4. Moving forward: Ask God for courage, and then share your story with a trusted friend this week. Ask your friend for encouragement and prayer—and offer the same.

Chapter 9: Waiting with Grace

1. Although most of us are still waiting for something, the grace we receive in our trials is knowing that God

is with us in the waiting. Have you ever experienced God's presence in the midst of struggle and pain?

2. As Christians, we have the grace of the Holy Spirit dwelling inside us forever. How can that truth change our perspective on waiting?

3. Ann says that the healing we long for here and now is "only a shadow of the full healing that will come in the new heaven and the new earth" (pages 195–96). How does this broader perspective help us as we face unfulfilled longings and unanswered prayers?

4. Moving forward: Read Revelation 21:1-5, and ask God to fill you with hope for the full healing and wholeness that will come when we reach our heavenly home.

Chapter 10: Hope for the Waiting Ones

1. The book of Hebrews tells us that hope and faith are inextricably intertwined: we can't have faith without hope (see Hebrews 11:1). If you had to measure the amount of hope you have right now on a scale of 1 to 10, where would your hope fall? Why?

2. Ann writes that when our hope is placed in a person, in an opportunity, or in our own bodies, it will fail. But hope in Jesus and in his coming Kingdom will never disappoint. How can we continue to hope when our circumstances don't seem to be budging?

3. The Bleeding Woman experienced restoration with her community, with God, and with herself after her

encounter with Jesus. Which kind(s) of restoration are you in need of right now?

4. What new insights into the story of the Bleeding Woman have you gleaned from reading this book? What have you learned about what it looks like to wait well?

5. Moving forward: Ask God to restore you in every way you need it. Read 1 Peter 1:3-9, and ask the Lord to give you the "joy that is inexpressible and filled with glory" as you wait for him.

ABOUT THE AUTHOR

ANN SWINDELL is a writer, speaker, and teacher who is passionate about seeing women set free by the love of Christ. She writes for multiple publications and makes her home in the Midwest with her husband and daughter. Ann holds an MA in writing from DePaul University and an MFA in creative nonfiction writing from Seattle Pacific University. She taught composition and creative writing courses as a college instructor for five years and now teaches an online writing course, Writing with Grace, at www.writingwithgrace.com. She loves helping other writers communicate clearly and powerfully as they seek to tell their own stories well.

You can get to know Ann more at www.annswindell.com.

AS YOU'RE WAITING,
DON'T WAIT ALONE.

Join us as we trust God in the middle
of our waiting seasons by sharing
our stories and using the hashtag
#stillwaitingbook
on Instagram, Facebook, and Twitter.

Then, connect with Ann
for more encouragement, hope, and truth!

CONNECT

@annswindell
www.annswindell.com